Unexpected
JOURNEYS

A Collection of Meditations and Prayers

Eddie Askew

By the same author:
A Silence and A Shouting
Disguises of Love
Many Voices One Voice
No Strange Land
Facing the Storm
Breaking the Rules
Cross Purposes
Slower than Butterflies
Music on the Wind
Edge of Daylight
Talking with Hedgehogs (book and spoken word cassette)

Published by
The Leprosy Mission International
80 Windmill Road, Brentford
Middlesex TW8 0QH, United Kingdom

Editorial and Design by Craft Plus Publishing Ltd.
53 Crown Street, Brentwood, Essex CM14 4BD
Printed and bound in Spain by Bookprint, S.L. - Barcelona
A catalogue record for this book is available from the British Library.
ISBN 0 902731 46 7

Cover picture (printed in full on pages 32-33): Sunshine after Storm, *Pastel*
Title page: Misty Morning, Lakes, *Watercolour*

Contents

Dedication

Once again to Barbara who has been with me
every step of the journey

Foreword

Nine years ago I stepped into the job that Eddie Askew had been doing until he retired from The Leprosy Mission in 1987. Coming as an outsider to the organisation I had only known Eddie through his writings. These have always been thought provoking, reflective, sometimes entertaining, but always a source of great inspiration.

Over recent years I have come to know Eddie personally and continue to find encouragement and challenge in his work. In a few lines of poetry and prose, or with the colourful strokes of a brush, Eddie can bring a freshness and new insight into otherwise familiar Biblical passages. He has an unnerving capacity to anchor them solidly in the common experiences of life and challenge our comfort zones.

Unexpected Journeys is no exception. Its insights, its verse, and the beautiful illustrations featuring Eddie's own pastels and watercolours can hardly fail to inspire and encourage you. As we each travel our own journeys through life, Eddie's work will help us to negotiate its pitfalls and stresses. It may even help you to start your own unexpected journey and discover a new world of hope and joy. May God open our eyes and minds as we enjoy this work.

Trevor Durston
General Director
The Leprosy Mission International

Introduction

Writing this book I've had a problem with the tenses. As I worked my way into the Bible stories they became so real, so vivid, I found myself slipping into the present tense as I began to write about them. The events were happening now, before my eyes. I was part of the scene, sharing in the awe, the excitement, the joy, the fear. The stories hit home because their truths are universal.

I thank God for imagination. He blessed us with it, it's there in our genes, but many of us let it atrophy through lack of use. It needs to be used with care. Fantasizing isn't part of it, but to put yourself into the story, to become a living part of it, opens doors into a new world. Read a story, imagine yourself there, take on a character and feel the emotions. Use all your senses. See the people. Feel the crowd pushing, smell the sea air, the fish and the sweat. Taste the water from the well, hear the voices.

Listen to what's said, and then listen for what isn't said and wonder why. Try to get behind the recorded words to the reality as it was being lived at the moment it was happening. Ask questions. God's comfortable with questions. Sometimes he answers them but not always. There's still a wonderful mystery about God, aspects of his nature no amount of story telling or imagination will ever capture, but it's permissible, and rewarding to try.

There's no set way to use this book. Use it your way – and use it with your imagination.

Eddie Askew

Looking at the paintings

My paintings are not so much about showing places; more about catching moods. Not *moodiness* in the way we often use that word but capturing my response to the wonder and beauty of God's creativity. I use the word creativity rather than creation because I believe it to be a continuing and continual process, not a once-and-for-all event.

In one painting I may try to suggest a feeling of tranquillity or struggle, calm or storm, joy or thankfulness.

Looking at paintings we all respond differently. Some pictures speak to us, others don't. To use these paintings as a help in your prayer time, I suggest that you get comfortable and look at a picture with some care.

Autumn Oaks   *Pastel*

Take time. First describe the scene to yourself, look at what's in it, note the colours, the light and shade, and the atmosphere. In quiet continue to look at it. Does it say anything to you? Perhaps it reminds you of something you've seen, an experience you've had.

Autumn Lake   *Watercolour*

Still Waters   *Watercolour*

Some element in the painting may start a train of thought which you can follow. An open gate can suggest freedom, a thorny hedge may remind you of a frustration you face. You may respond to the colour of the painting. Don't push it too hard, and don't feel you must drive your thoughts to a conclusion.

Finally, turn your mind and feelings towards God and open your heart to anything he may want to say to you through the picture. It may be a simple thank you; it may be a challenge, or something deeper. It may even suggest there's something you need to do. Only you will know.

Bright Day, Isle of Mull   *Gouache*

Thimpu Dzong, Bhutan   *Watercolour*

If a particular painting doesn't speak to you, don't worry. Perhaps the next one will. And if this form of prayer doesn't work for you, try something else. We are all different, and God glories in our individuality.

Eddie Askew

Part One

Holy Ground

Sunshine after Storm   *Pastel*

Reading – Exodus 3:1-12

Now Moses was tending the flocks of Jethro his father-in-law, the priest of Midian, and he led the flock to the far side of the desert and came to Horeb, the mountain of God. There the angel of the Lord appeared to him in flames of fire from within a bush. Moses saw that though the bush was on fire it did not burn up. So Moses thought, "I will go over and see this strange sight – why the bush does not burn up."

When the Lord saw that he had gone over to look, God called to him from within the bush, "Moses, Moses."

And Moses said, "Here I am."

"Do not come any closer," God said. "Take off your sandals, for the place where you are standing is holy ground." Then he said, "I am the God of your father, the God of Abraham, the God of Isaac and the God of Jacob." At this, Moses hid his face, because he was afraid to look at God.

The Lord said, "I have indeed seen the misery of my people in Egypt. I have heard them crying out because of their slave drivers, and I am concerned about their suffering. So I have come down to rescue them from the hand of the Egyptians and to bring them up out of that land into a good and spacious land, a land flowing with milk and honey – the home of the Canaanites, Hittites, Amorites, Perrizites, Hivites and Jebusites. And now the cry of the Israelites has reached me, and I have seen the way the Egyptians are oppressing them. So now, go. I am sending you to Pharoah to bring my people the Israelites out of Egypt."

But Moses said to God, "Who am I, that I should go to Pharaoh and bring the Israelites out of Egypt?"

And God said, "I will be with you. And this will be a sign to you that it is I who have sent you: When you have brought the people out of Egypt, you will worship God on this mountain."

Imagine...

The sun hurts the eyes, its dry heat sears the skin.
It drains all colour from the sky.
There is no cloud, just a pale featureless glare
from horizon to horizon. The desert lies defeated in the heat.
Great cliffs of red rock, sharp-edged, skeletal, forbidding.
Deep violet shadows etch lines across stony ground,
the monotony punctuated by a forlorn line
of scrubby thorn bushes clinging to life.

A track, almost invisible, twists through the wadi,
a memory of streams of water long gone.
All is still; no birds sing. The silence is profound,
except for one distant sound, so faint it might not exist at all.
Then it comes again, carrying softly through the still air.
It's the bleat of a goat. A small black dot forms, grows larger.
More dots appear, coalesce, break apart,
shimmering in the heat. A flock of sheep and goats.
They walk slowly, nosing among the stones, cropping the few
sparse plants that survive close to the ground.

With them is another figure, upright, human.
He too walks slowly, conserving energy.
He carries a heavy staff in his hand, a cloth bundle
and a skin of water across his back.
His worn robe is of rough, brown cloth, homespun
from the wool of the animals. He is alert, fit,
thinned down by the diet and exertion
of nomadic life in the desert.
His skin is burnt brown by sun and wind,
his shoulder-length hair streaked and bleached.
His hands are strong and there
is dirt under his fingernails. He is Moses.

He follows the track, the stones rough
under his feet, looking for a precious
landmark that will lead his flock to water.
Suddenly he stops, grasps his staff more firmly,
his attention riveted by something he has seen.
A sudden glint of light, a flicker of flame.
Flame usually means people, and wandering

nomads aren't always friendly.
He slowly scans the landscape, looking into the shadows,
alert for sound or movement. There is none.
He is alone with his flock.

The flame flickers again, glows brighter.
A bush burns among a jumble of rocks.
Still holding his staff Moses moves quietly,
slowly, towards it. At first he is cautious,
then curious, puzzled. This is strange.
Bushes in the desert are tinder dry,
they burn up quickly in a rush and crackle of heat,
and only ash remains. But this bush is different.
As he nears it his curiosity turns to awe.
There is a strange tension in the air,
like nothing he has ever experienced.
A shiver runs down his spine in spite of the heat.
Instinctively he steps out of his sandals.
There is a sound, so faint as to be part of the silence.
A voice, which could be from the bush or could be
in his mind, calls his name, "Moses, Moses."

Now Moses was tending the flocks of Jethro
his father-in-law,
the priest of Midian...

Exodus 3:1

Teenage years are always a time of doubt and questioning. Brought up in
the culture of the Egyptian court, but knowing his background as a
foundling from the river, Moses had more questions than most boys.
Who was he? Where did he belong? I don't know how far teenage
rebellion was tolerated in his adoptive family but testosterone was a fact
of life, then as now, and his emotions weren't always under control.

He must have grown into a powerful young man. Egyptian princes were
trained to hunt in the marshes of the Nile and in the surrounding desert.
They learned hands-on weapon skills, with bow and arrow, javelin and
bronze sword. But still there must have been unresolved tensions pulling
him apart, his Hebrew heritage struggling with his Egyptian upbringing.
Years later the feelings erupted in one great surge of anger, a moment of
violence that changed his life. He killed a foreman who was bullying
Moses' own people and hid the body in the sand but his crime was soon
revealed and Moses fled into the desert.

The murder, for that's what it was, is something we gloss over in our
reading. We prefer to see it as an outburst of righteous anger, and move
on to the great adventure of the rest of Moses' life. But we need to pause
and think. Can we envisage a God of love in partnership with Moses,
willing him to murder? No amount of piety can work round that. It's far
too simplistic a viewpoint. Moses' crime and the death of the overseer
must have grieved God as much as the Israelites' suffering grieved him.
God has no favourites; Egyptians were as precious to him as Hebrews.
And Palestinians as precious as Israelis.

But God can take the unpromising circumstances of life, whether they are
within his will or not, and weave them into good. That doesn't make the
initial actions right but it can transform them. That's what happened in
Moses' experience. Exchanging the luxury of Egypt for the hard life of a
wandering shepherd didn't seem to be a step up but it was only a
beginning. And as he runs for his life God goes with him every step of the
journey, as he does with us.

Always there, Lord?
Wherever I go, whatever I do?
I know it's meant to comfort
but there are times I feel like curling up
and hiding in a corner.
Hiding from you? You most of all.
I find it hard
to fit your holiness around my life
or shape my life into your holiness.
I'd rather grab a comfort blanket of indifference
and, thumb in mouth,
pretend that you're not there.
The part you play within my life
is meant for good – and works for good.
I know that's true
but lurking in the darkness of my being
still lie the seeds of anger
that can grow with Jack-and-beanstalk speed
at smallest provocation.
And then I need you near,
not just to bless but overrule
and get me back on track.
Then, peace restored,
or near as I can get to that,
I realise you can take my anger,
absorb the violence inside,
Reshape it into energy
and redirect the journey
through my self-created desert
towards the promised land.
The way is long, signposts are few,
but strengthened by your love
I realise with joy
that all I am and all I do,
imperfect though it is,
can be of use to you.
Stay with me, Lord, keep close
especially when it seems
I'm telling you to go away.
Then, most of all.

> ...and he led the flock to the far side of
> the desert and came to Horeb, the mountain of God.
>
> Exodus 3:1

Moses was leading the flock from one water hole to the next. He was a tough, purposeful, resourceful man. As I watch him I try to see into his mind, imagine his thoughts. He'd many things to be thankful for. First, he was still alive. He'd escaped from Egypt and, as far as Pharaoh was concerned, had disappeared in the desert. Then he'd found a home and a wife in the extended family of Jethro. I'm sure it was an arranged marriage to Zipporah but I hope it blossomed into love, although that's something we can never know. And now they had a son to cherish.

Moses also had a livelihood as a shepherd. A responsible job – the wealth of most nomadic tribes is tied up in its animals – but I wonder how fulfilling Moses found it. It's hard to believe that this quiet and frugal life could be sufficient challenge for a strong, dynamic and highly intelligent man. A flock of goats and sheep isn't the most exciting responsibility there is. How did he pass the time, walking and watching in the wilderness? What occupied his mind? Perhaps thoughts of Egypt, the good friends and the luxury of life at court conflicting with the heartache of remembering his own people, the Israelites with whom he'd identified himself so violently. They were still suffering and the thought must have nagged away at him. Did he regret the killing which had sent his whole life spinning out of control? He had plenty of time to face what he'd done and come to terms with it – we're told it was a long period (Exodus 2:23) – but there still seemed no purpose in it. Just a great mistake.

Moses was facing the pain of change. Radical, unsettling, heart-wrenching change. He'd made a dramatic journey from the Egyptian delta to the black tents of nomadic Bedouin. It had turned his whole life upside down and Moses had no idea where it would end. There was no career plan carefully mapped out and projected years ahead with a pension invested. Just a blank, and God seemed content to leave it like that. To allow Moses to sweat it out, literally and spiritually, in the wilderness. Some wadis twist and turn through the rocks and end up in a cul-de-sac. No way through. That's where Moses seemed to be. There must have been times when he felt abandoned, but the journey of the spirit always has to be made alone, and maybe it was the emptiness in his life that made Moses sensitive enough to recognise the presence of the Lord.

In her deeply moving book When the Heart Waits * Sue Monk Kidd describes an acute crisis in her life. Nothing was going right and she was near despair. One day she found a chrysalis in a dogwood tree. The cocoon seemed lifeless, yet she realised that profound change was happening inside it and that in a few short months new life would emerge. It told her that waiting is an essential part of spiritual growth, painful and unpredictable though it may be.

Waiting can be hard. Desert experiences aren't pleasant but impatience gets us nowhere except deeper into frustration. The only thing we can do is wait, and pray through the darkness. God had his purpose for Moses as he has for us, and he makes it clear when he's good and ready, and not before.

Published by Harper and Row, San Francisco 1990

I've known the desert, Lord,
explored the vacant spaces of my life
and stood, hands empty,
with nothing to offer you but tears.
Lost in the wilderness,
following the tracks of my own will
and finding no oasis.
Only dried-out river beds,
the water of life evaporated
in the heat of my desires.

I've called to you so many times,
sought you in desperation
and heard my voice bounce back unanswered.
Or so it seemed.
But through the years
I've learnt to wait –
a lesson, Lord, that's hard –
and realise that battering on your door
will only hurt my hands and do no good.

And in my more enlightened moments –
not many, I admit –
I understand there is no need to struggle,
just find the patience and the faith to wait –
both hard for me to do –
and learn the emptiness I feel
is one more stage upon my pilgrimage.
A space you carve
to give yourself a home in me.

It may be painful and bewildering at times
but in the end there'll come a day
when I can look along the track I've come
and thank you for your presence
even when I've told myself
that you weren't there.
Meanwhile, I'll take another breath
and wait some more.

Violet and Gold

Pastel

> There the angel of the Lord appeared to him
> in flames of fire from within a bush. Moses saw
> that though the bush was on fire it did not burn up.
> So Moses thought, "I will go over and see this strange sight –
> why the bush does not burn up."
>
> Exodus 3:2-3

Leaders rarely come ready-made. In those waiting times when life seemed purposeless and filled only with the bleat of hungry, thirsty animals God was sowing seeds in the soil of Moses' life. Moments and moods of uncertainty, frustration and discomfort. (The Holy Spirit is called the comforter in some Bible translations (John 19:16) but in my life he's as often been the discomforter, the one who has challenged my assumptions, shaken up my easy beliefs and opened my horizons to fresh truth.) The seeds started to germinate and take root in Moses' mind. Thoughts of the suffering of his people in Egypt were beginning to surface. God was creating a longing, a deep inarticulate desire for a sense of purpose in his life.

Suddenly the waiting was over in a flickering of flame. The mysterious bush focused Moses' attention. People often describe deep spiritual experiences in terms of fire. This description can only have come from Moses himself. No one else was there at the bush except the sheep and the goats, and they weren't talking. Later he must have struggled to find words to describe the indescribable to the people he led. It was his own Pentecost as the Spirit descended in tongues of flame and burned God's purpose into his life. We tend to be more at ease with gentler images of God, as father, lover, provider. Moses experienced his presence as flame, burning, purifying, at times frightening. Yet that flame was only a small indication of the power of God; just strong enough to change Moses, but not so strong as to overwhelm him. A great volcanic outpouring of fire would have been too much. God measures out his revelation in terms of what we can bear. Centuries later the two disciples whom Jesus befriended on the road to Emmaus felt a gentler heat. "Were not our hearts burning within us while he talked with us on the road?" they asked. (Luke 24:32)

The bush burned but it wasn't consumed. That's a truth I hang on to. God's fire doesn't destroy. It incinerates the dross but leaves us whole. God's fire recreates; more the purpose of a pottery kiln than a garden bonfire. Moses went forward, his curiosity drawing him to the bush. That's revealing too. He went to look. He could have stayed at a distance or turned away. There was no compulsion. Moses had a choice. God always gives us a choice, that's an essential part of the freedom he offers, but think of what Moses would have missed if he'd used his freedom to turn away. The prodigal returned to the father.

And incidentally I wonder what the goats and sheep were doing while all this was happening. I imagine they went on grazing among the rocks, getting on with their ordinary lives unaware of the cosmic drama unfolding around them. How easy it is for us to live through the momentous and the miraculous without recognising it.

Lord, open my eyes
to the wonder of your presence.
I long for you
and though some say
the longing is the proof
that you're already in my life
it's still so easy to get mired in the ordinary.
To walk, eyes down,
horizons hemmed, vision restricted,
and blinkered to the glory all around.
Cords of routine tying me down
a little at a time,
till I can't turn my head,
and my life in you is more a future promise
than a present truth.

Please help me, Lord
to feel the fire of your love,
to feel it now,
a spark that gathers to a flame.
To see the bush burn bright,
blaze into life,
and in the momentary sear of heat
to hear your voice
calling my name.
Not to face pharaohs –
I'm not prepared for that just yet –
but to find the strength to live the little heroisms
that daily life demands.
To live your love
in everything I do.

Please help me, Lord,
to feel the fire of your love,
to see the bush burn bright
and blaze into life.

Far Horizons, Norfolk

Watercolour

> "Take off your sandals,
> for the place where you are standing is holy ground."
>
> Exodus 3:5

Someone was calling Moses' name. Was it a voice echoing around the mountainside or was it a still small voice in his mind, gentle but persistent? I don't know and I don't believe it matters. What mattered was that Moses was being drawn deeper, lovingly but firmly, into the presence of God. What Brother Lawrence, writing in the 17th century, describes in The Practice of the Presence of God as 'the fire of holy love'. Some mysteries are too deep for us to know, that's why they're called mysteries. It was a personal encounter with a God who knew his name. Moses didn't yet know God's name, he'd ask about that a little later in the story, but God knew his. God had a place in his plans for Moses, the man with dirt under his fingernails, and blood on his hands. The reasons for God's choices aren't always obvious and he rarely takes time to enlighten me. There are occasions when I disagree with God's choice but before I get too critical he reminds me to take a long look at myself. That usually brings me down to earth. And that's where Moses was, standing on the stony ground near the bush.

Instinctively he took off his sandals, an action deep in the human psyche. Whatever the religion, worshippers have a tradition of entering the temple, the mosque, barefoot. Throughout Asia Christians still do it, a gesture of humility we in the West have lost. But then we've lost most of our humility in the 21st century and it would help us regain it if we could recognise and acknowledge God's presence in our lives even though we may never fully understand it.

I have a problem though with this concept of holy ground, the idea that some places are holier than others. It's hard to define. Where do we draw the boundary round the burning bush? Could Moses step forward and back, one moment on holy ground, the next moment not? It seems to me that holy ground isn't a church, a shrine or a place of pilgrimage. There are places, 'thin places' as George Macleod called them, 'with only a bit of tissue paper between things spiritual and things material'*, where God's presence is almost tangible. But it is his presence that is holy, not the place If that's true, and I believe it is, then everywhere is holy ground because God is everywhere. God was there when Moses was hidden as a baby at the river's edge, in Pharaoh's court, in the oasis and the desert; even present when Moses killed the Egyptian overseer, although his presence didn't mean consent.

For us the market and the workplace are as holy as the church, for that's where God is with us. The desk we sit at may not burst into flame like the bush, although in his poem God's Grandeur Gerald Manley Hopkins saw the world, 'shining like shook foil' with God's presence. Our supermarket trolley may not glow incandescently but God's there, calling us by name to acknowledge his closeness and to claim our lives.

As Moses stepped out of his worn, dusty sandals he was suddenly, startlingly aware of the God who had been with him unrecognised all the time. A God who sanctified the place with his presence. A God who sanctifies where we are because that's where he is.

* Quoted by John Rackley in Thin Places, Open House Publications 1999

Autumn Oaks   *Pastel*

I am no Moses, Lord
that much is obvious
but still I long
for the awakening,
the moment when I hear your voice
and find my burning bush,
bright-shining in the desert.
To share an instant
on that holy ground of intimacy,
the world ignored, all else excluded.
The moment when, sandals removed,
my barefoot spirit
stands alone with you
and we can share the stillness with each other.

Meanwhile I struggle on,
not leading goats or sheep
– although it sometimes feels that way
when I've survived the desert
of a tedious meeting –
but facing the routine day after day,
doing my best
to see some meaning in it all.
And straining still to hear your voice
– so still, so small –
not in the silence
but within the clamour of my life,
where everything shouts loud
and meaning's lost in pandemonium.
But as I wait
alert to any sign of flame
perhaps the problem is
I talk too much and listen less.
Your holy ground is all around me,
your voice in those who ask for help.
And maybe
if I stilled my mind
I'd find the flashpoint,
and the damp tinder
of my commitment
would be fanned to fire again.

> "I am the God of your father, the God of Abraham,
> the God of Isaac and the God of Jacob."
>
> Exodus 3:6

In this moment at the burning bush Moses must have lost touch with everything outside himself, his sudden awareness of God's overwhelming presence sweeping in. A moment of ecstasy when the world was concentrated into a single point of light in which God was the only reality. Nothing else mattered. In that moment God was everything.

As the moment of ecstasy moved on to rational thought, God put Moses' experience into context. "This isn't just for you and me, Moses," he says, "I'm not your personal discovery. I am the God of your fathers..." I'm making up this bit of the dialogue, but the point is that God was relating Moses' experience to the whole community of his people.

It's so easy to take religious experience in isolation, particularly today where some folk seem to deny the concept of society and place value only on the individual. Easy to assume that what happens to me is unique, that no one has ever had quite the revelation that I've had, and to wear it as a mark of my superiority. It's true that each person's encounter with God is an individual encounter, as was Moses', but it isn't meant to stay that way. My encounter with God is meant for my good but it isn't meant to separate me from other people nor to give me any special privileges.

Personal renewal will take us back into the Christian community – and through that into the wider world – renewed and with a clearer sense of purpose. God was the God of Moses' ancestors and of all his people, and as Moses was a small part of their living history so are we part of our own society. And amazingly the God of Moses and his people is our God too. There's a continuity to God's presence and activity in the world that we don't always acknowledge and value as we might. The temptation today may be to interpret and limit our experience to 'God and me' and, God forgive us, with the me first. Not so, says the Lord, this revelation has a wider purpose.

God gave Moses a job to do. A job which frightened him because it seemed so far beyond his power and ability, and the only reassurance Moses got was the promise that God would be with him. Maybe not always in the spectacular (although there was to be a pillar of fire which led him later) but in a daily strengthening as he struggled to carry out God's will.

Lord, in the history of your world
I find it hard to think
I have a role of any great significance.
Yet there's a grandeur in it all
a sense of presence
and of purpose.
Impossible to grasp
yet definitely there.
A trail of wonder shining through my life,
intriguing and frustrating,
brighter and dim by turns,
its splendour clear then clouded.
Yet through it all, the dark and light,
I sense an awesome continuity,
a power and a constant strength
that I can't comprehend.
All I can do is stand and praise you.
The exhilarating truth
that you are here with me
and that there is a place for me
within your purposes
is great beyond my understanding.
But if you really do count sparrows as the story says,
it must be true that I am valued
– not to make me think I'm better than the rest in any way
although I'm prone to that at times –
but so that my small talents can be used
to make a contribution to the building of your kingdom.
A kingdom where I stand
not with the stature of a Moses
but as a part of your great family,
throughout the ages.
Loved and accepted
not for what I've done
but for who you are.

"So now, go. I am sending you to Pharaoh to bring my people the Israelites out of Egypt." 'But Moses said to God,' "Who am I, that I should go to Pharaoh` and bring the Israelites out of Egypt?"' And God said, "I will be with you."

Exodus 3:10-12

His encounter with God wasn't meant to boost Moses' ego. It was to give him a mission. I think encounters with God always are. Richard Holloway says, "With the experience of the divine mystery comes a sense that something is required of us."* The intimate moment of meeting leads to a public commitment. Responsibility follows revelation. My responsibility may not have the earth-shaking significance that Moses' had but it can't be avoided, although that's just what Moses tried to do. And so do I, given half a chance.

Moses put up as many objections as he could. His lack of position or power, his doubts about whether his people in Egypt would listen to him, his slowness of thought and speech. Modesty may be a virtue but playing down and undervaluing our abilities to avoid responsibility isn't.

But there are two questions within this interplay with God, and Moses asked them both. "Who am I?" and "Who are you?" Basic questions in all human relationships and particularly in our relationship with God. Or maybe they are two sides of the same question.

"Who am I?" As I sit and stare at my computer screen I still ask that question and the truthful answer is "Only God knows." I can define myself in relation to my family, my colleagues, my friends. I can see parts of myself in my writing and painting but only God knows who I truly am. Whatever behavioural psychologists may say, I am largely an unknown quantity with depths only God can penetrate. And ultimately who I am is meaningful only in my relationship with him, even though it is expressed through my relationships with my family and other people.

The second question is even simpler and yet more complex. When Moses asked God "What is your name?" he was asking about the very nature of God. In Moses' day names weren't just a convenient handle for identification, they implied character, and a certain power came with knowing someone's name. In his question Moses mirrored the search and predicament of every believer. He was asking for certainty, a money-back guarantee on God's nature, but he didn't get it. God replied with the demands of faith. All he would say was "I will be with you."

Confirmation would come after the event. That had to be enough for Moses and has to be enough for us.

However close our encounter with God in burning bush, or quiet meeting, or in our daily living, he remains a mystery. A loving mystery rather than a threatening one. George Appleton, once bishop in Jerusalem, wrote

> *I cannot grasp you*
> *explain you*
> *describe you*
> *Only cast myself into the depths of your mystery.* * *

In an age where science provides us with so much information about the world we live in we assume that we have a right to know everything, but God simply says, "Trust me." It worked for Moses even as it turned his life upside down. Life is always turned upside down when you trust God but many of us would say that faith really turns life back the right way up!

* *Dancing on the Edge by Richard Holloway, published by Fount Paperbacks 1997*
** *The Oxford Book of Prayer OUP 1985. Quoted in Furnace of the Heart by Margaret Magdalen CSMV*

Who am I, Lord?
I ask the question as I've asked it many times before.
Asked it in joy on starry nights
when I have wondered at the beauty of your universe
and gloried that I'm part of it.
Asked it on misty mornings
when anxiety has ruled and I could see no way ahead.
And as I ask it yet again
the pendulum of my thoughts swings wild.
One moment I'm the prodigal returned,
the next the prodigal still wasting life
in ways I wouldn't want to talk about.
And in the clamour of my questioning
there's little room for your reply.
It's only when I stop and wait and listen
that your voice comes clear,
its promise firm
and I am reassured that you are with me.
And then I realise, as Moses did,
that I'm defined in you as part of your creation.
Something, someone you love and treasure
and will not abandon
however much I doubt or question.

And who are you, Lord?
That's harder to define but much more to the point.
There was a time of youthful dogmatism
when I thought I knew just who you were,
and could contain you
in my goldfish bowl of understanding.

Yet now I know you better
I realise I know you less.
I only know there's more to know
than I can ever grasp.
You are the breadth and length
and depth of infinite love
released into the world.
Released into my life,
your nature seeded into mine,
transforming, oh so slowly,
what I am to what I'm meant to be.
Your perfect love taking my imperfection
and remoulding it,
sometimes in pain, sometimes in joy,
and leading me along the way
towards a final consummation.
I am content, as much as I will ever be,
and when you tell me where to go
and what to do
I'll try to trust you more
and question less.

You are the breadth
and length and depth
of infinite love
released into the world.

Sunshine after Storm
Pastel

Part Two

Living through Change

Morecambe Bay   *Watercolour*

Reading – Ruth 1:1-19

In the days when the judges ruled, there was a famine in the land, and a man from Bethlehem in Judah, together with his wife and two sons, went to live for a while in the country of Moab. The man's name was Elimelech, his wife's name Naomi, and the names of his two sons were Mahlon and Kilion. They were Ephrathites from Bethlehem, Judah. And they went to Moab and lived there.

Now Elimelech, Naomi's husband, died, and she was left with her two sons. They married Moabite women, one named Orpah and the other Ruth. After they had lived there about ten years, both Mahlon and Kilion also died, and Naomi was left without her two sons and her husband.

When she heard in Moab that the Lord had come to the aid of his people by providing food for them, Naomi and her daughters-in-law prepared to return home from there. With her two daughters-in-law she left the place where she had been living and set out on the road that would take them back to the land of Judah.

Then Naomi said to her two daughters-in-law, "Go back, each of you, to your mother's home. May the Lord show kindness to you, as you have shown to your dead and to me. May the Lord grant that each of you will find rest in the home of another husband."

Then she kissed them and they wept aloud and said to her, "We will go back with you to your people."

But Naomi said, "Return home, my daughters. Why would you come with me? Am I going to have any more sons, who could become your husbands? Return home, my daughters; I am too old to have another husband. Even if I thought there was still hope for me – even if I had a husband tonight and then gave birth to sons – would you wait until they grew up? Would you remain unmarried for them? No, my daughters. It is more bitter for me than for you, because the Lord's hand has gone out against me!"

At this they wept again. Then Orpah kissed her mother-in-law goodbye, but Ruth clung to her. "Look," said Naomi, "your sister-in-law is going back to her own people and her gods. Go back with her."

But Ruth replied, "Don't urge me to leave you or to turn back from you. Where you go I will go, and where you stay I will stay. Your people will be my people, and your God my God. Where you die I will die, and there will I be buried. May the Lord deal with me, be it ever so severely, if anything but death separates you and me." When Naomi realised that Ruth was determined to go with her, she stopped urging her.

So the two women went on until they came to Bethlehem.

Imagine...

A refugee camp. Temporary shelters cover the ground, each fighting for space. They are built of anything that can be scavenged from the neighbourhood and recycled. Rough stones make low walls to stake a claim to a few square yards of ground. Precious branches from now denuded trees hold together a thin screen of dried palm leaves. The leaves rustle in the breeze, offering an illusion of privacy. Stretched over it all a square of ragged cloth makes a canopy and offers the only shade. There's dust everywhere. The shacks have no doors. Someone always has to stay to guard the few precious possessions each family has managed to carry from home. Narrow paths twist through the jumble.

It's a noisy place. Nerves are stretched and quarrels break out between reluctant neighbours over the ownership of a piece of wood. Dogs bark and scavenge for scraps. One yelps as it is driven away with a kick and a curse. Children cry, insecure, hungry, bored, not understanding why their lives have changed so dramatically. Some wander and get lost. There's occasional panic as parents search for them, calling their names. Inside many of the shelters old folk lie inert, lethargic, weak and exhausted by the journey. There are frequent outbursts of grief and many funerals.

Hanging over the camp are the smells. Of poverty, the stink of waste, the smoke of fires, occasionally the smell of cooking. Neither fuel nor food is easy to find. As more families arrive, worn and weary, clothes ragged and dirty, more shelters go up on the edge of the encampment, adding to the confusion. Water is precious – and heavy. Women and children struggle with dripping water pots as they carry them from the stream down the track. The days are hot but at night families huddle together for warmth under the few blankets they've been able to carry with them. There is an overwhelming sense of listlessness throughout the camp. People have lost everything. Homes and possessions, precious land. Above all, they have lost hope. There is nothing left but the struggle for survival in a strange land and culture.

> "...there was a famine in the land..."
>
> Ruth 1:1

It's hard at times to identify God's purposes. Piety sometimes ignores reality and pretends to a certainty it doesn't really possess. Do we try to discern a purpose in the famine and attribute it to God or do we accept it as a natural disaster in the hope that good can be salvaged from it? I choose the latter. To understand an Old Testament story we need the experience of a New Testament God. As a Scottish preacher, Thomas Allen, once said, "You have to read the Bible in big chunks otherwise you get it wrong."

Naomi and her family lived in Bethlehem. The name means House of Bread in Hebrew, House of Meat in Arabic. In whatever language, the name suggests it was a productive area. Until the rains failed. That meant poor harvests. Food supplies dwindled. Families ate the seed they were saving for the next spring sowing. People began to die, the old and the very young. There were family arguments about whether to stay or leave; whether it was better to die at home or risk everything by heading into the unknown. Naomi, her husband and two sons faced the challenge of an unexpected journey. They joined a growing trail of refugees heading east into the Jordan valley, across the river and around the northern fringe of the Dead Sea. They carried what they could – their sleeping mats, cooking pots, bundles of clothing and an occasional piece of treasured jewellery carefully hidden. They travelled fearfully to Moab, unsure of their welcome. Israelites and Moabites were traditional enemies, hostile and suspicious of each other. The present was a time of uneasy peace; their reception might be civil, it would not be warm.

The refugees were ordinary people, the sort of people whose lives are always disrupted by famine or war, the powerless and voiceless who suffer in any calamity. Even in those circumstances it took courage to leave behind everything they knew for a future that was unsettled, possibly dangerous, certainly unclear. That's how life often is and it's not always easy to find reassurance in the hope that it's all within God's will. Good may come out of suffering. Sometimes, looking back, we can see the truth of that but not always. There were years of uncertainty for Naomi; the grief and pain of losing home, husband and sons. Only much later did she find comfort and consolation in the love and companionship Ruth offered and she never knew that her life had played a significant part in God's plan. I call it comfort delayed and it demands great courage and stubborn faith to continue believing when life is so hard.

The uncertainty's not easy, Lord,
in fact at times it's almost unendurable.
There were no loaves and fishes on the road for them
as hunger drove them on their way.
And whether it's Naomi and her family
or those I watch so often on my television screen
it's much the same.
The drab, sad lines of stoic suffering, hiding the broken hearts,
the hopes tattered as the rags they wear,
ordinary people caught up in horrors they cannot control.
Facing the wrenching change that blows their world to bits
and reassembles it into a jigsaw-life of suffering.
Incomplete, with pieces missing.

Where are you, Lord, in this?
Where were you in Naomi's suffering?
I can't believe you caused the famine, Lord.
My gut reaction – or the Holy Spirit working in my life –
says that a God of love would never be so harsh
however good the outcome was to be.

There, Lord, I've had my moment of complaint,
let off the built-up steam,
and now I wait in hope of some enlightenment.
It's hard, the wait, until I hear an echo,
not of reasoned argument, but one small voice
that cuts right through my questioning
and says that you are with me always, and with them,
as long as life shall last and far beyond.
Walking and loving us along the road,
however hard that road may be.
Sharing the load, the pain, the insecurity
and, when the going's rough, suffering with us.

It's not an easy answer, Lord,
a suffering God,
but I am reassured that though the hardship
may not end for all,
and though at times our partnership with you
may be a partnership of pain,
at least you know the feel of it.
I'll leave it there, with you.

A love that offers everything,
holds nothing back
and leaps feet first
into an unknown future.

Golden Days, Lake District

> "Go back, each of you, to your mother's home."
>
> Ruth 1:8

Refugee camps are unpleasant places. I've visited famine and refugee camps in Bangladesh and Sudan. I've looked into the eyes of sick, hungry people and looked away again; the feeling of helplessness can be overwhelming.

Somehow Naomi and her family survived their famine. We don't know how long they stayed in their temporary accommodation but the story seems to suggest that eventually they found somewhere more permanent to settle. Then tragedy struck once more. Naomi's husband died. Perhaps from the strain of exile and caring for his family, maybe from illness or malnutrition. We're not told.

There seemed little hope then of a return to Judah so her two sons settled down with Moabite wives. I wonder how their Moabite in-laws felt about their daughters marrying outside the tribe? Yet more tension to strain family ties. It would be comforting to think that Naomi found some contentment in the marriages and looked forward to grandchildren, but there's no mention of any. Far from it. Within a few years both her sons were dead too. Moab had become a place of sorrow for her and when news came that the famine in Judah was over she decided to leave and go home – to whatever was left of it.

Naomi had to make hard decisions but she was a strong woman. She prepared to make another sacrifice by persuading her daughters-in-law to stay in their own country. She knew what it was like to be a foreigner in a strange land and didn't want them to suffer as she had. Parting would have meant loneliness for her, with no support either on the journey back or during her resettlement in Bethlehem, but it seemed the better of poor alternatives.

Doubt and fear are never mentioned but surely they were part of the story. It's human to feel anxious and more heroic to work through the fear than to pretend it isn't there. I'm sure Naomi had her times of doubt when faith was hard to cling to. Orpah felt it and agreed to stay in Moab, but Ruth wouldn't listen. "Where you go, I'll go," she said through her tears. Naomi struggled with her own feelings, half of her wanting Ruth to go with her, the other half trying to persuade her to stay. "Where you go, I'll go." The words must have stirred echoes in Naomi's mind and heart. She would have said similar things to her husband all those years before when the famine struck and they had decided to leave Judah as a family. Now Ruth was saying them as another journey was about to begin. There would be no certainties on the road and no guarantee of what they would find at journey's end. Yet Ruth was willing to face it. One sacrifice inspires another, and love begets love. And Ruth's commitment to Naomi mirrors God's commitment to each of us. Where we go, he will go and he will never leave us.

It's tempting, Lord
to stay at home
when faced with hard decisions.
To turn my back,
stay rooted in the soil of what I know
rather than look uncertainty right in the face,
although I think uncertainty has many faces
– or none – I'm not quite sure.

The world out there can seem so threatening,
the changes rapid, unexpected.
A frightened fledgling,
I'd rather nest in what I know,
than risk my wings in flight.
The nest is warm and undemanding
but its safety is unreal
and soon outgrown,
security as insubstantial
as the air I'm frightened of.
And staying home
would breed a poverty of spirit
more dangerous than the journey.
Help me to find the courage, Lord,
to launch out into space
wherever you may lead.
To widen my horizons,
soar with confidence,
explore the possibilities
of life and love with you.
Take to the air on wings of faith
and fly.

But Ruth replied, "Don't urge me to leave you or to turn back from you. Where you go I will go, and where you stay I will stay. Your people will be my people and your God my God. Where you die I will die and there will I be buried."

Ruth 1:16-17

Naomi must have been a good mother-in-law. She inspired love, or so Ruth's decision suggests. Faced with the choice of staying with the familiar or moving into unknown territory, Ruth elected to go. Naomi exerted no pressure on Ruth to go with her. Rather the pressure was for her to stay where she was, but Ruth wouldn't hear of it. The cynic might say that she wouldn't have had much of a life going back to her own family after marrying an alien but she would be going to Bethlehem as an alien in her own right, which could have been worse. This was a serious case of love. Orpah doesn't get such a good press but maybe the thought of exchanging everything she knew for a completely unknown lifestyle was too daunting for her, her courage overwhelmed by doubt.

But not Ruth. She was so committed to Naomi that she was ready to give up everything for her. No, that's the wrong way of putting it. The Bible story is very positive. It doesn't talk about what Ruth gave up but what she gained. In leaving Moab she would gain a new people, a new God and a new future. And it would last for life and beyond. With hindsight we can see what Ruth couldn't see and we know what her future held. Through her marriage to Boaz she would become part of a family chain that would move on to King David and through him to Jesus himself.

The whole story tells of commitment. It's a relationship that transcends race and nationality. It doesn't exactly devalue tradition and background; it sees them as baggage that may be useful in giving us an identity but can be discarded when situations change and personal relationships offer a choice.

And I hope it's not straining the story too far to see it as a metaphor of faith. Faith freely entered into and bringing, even through subsequent questioning and hardship, a future that could never have been defined in advance. Faith may ask us to put some parts of our life behind us and to move out without a detailed itinerary, as Moses was asked to do at the burning bush. There's an excitement and adventure about our unexpected journeys if we have the courage to stake the future on them. Faith asks us to move on, not because we think we'll gain more than we'll lose but because of the love that inspires it.

I can't resist quoting Ruth's words again, but this time from the King James' version with its lovely cadences: "Intreat me not to leave thee, or to return from following after thee: for whither thou goest I will go; and where thou lodgest I will lodge: thy people shall be my people, and thy God my God: Where thou diest, will I die, and there will I be buried..."

I stand before you, Lord,
the words I would have spoken
better left unsaid.
I cannot claim commitment
of the magnitude of Ruth's.
My own is weak, battered by life
and all my many failures.
It leaves me gasping, Lord,
a love like that.
A love that offers everything,
holds nothing back and leaps feet first
into an unknown future.

But as I pause and think and wait
I begin to sense the courage and the pain
within the love.
And then my eyes are opened
and I move from her to you.
I see her love an echo of your own,
and hear you quietly reminding me
that that's what Jesus did.
Left home for love.
Gave life for love.
Gave everything for love of me.
And in the words she spoke,
I hear his voice assuring me
that in my life's adventure he is always there.
Where I go he will go,
where I stay he will stay,
and that – if you'll allow a paraphrase –
we shall be one in you, our God.
The only difference is
that death will never part us
and in the life that follows death
you'll still be there.
Alleluia!

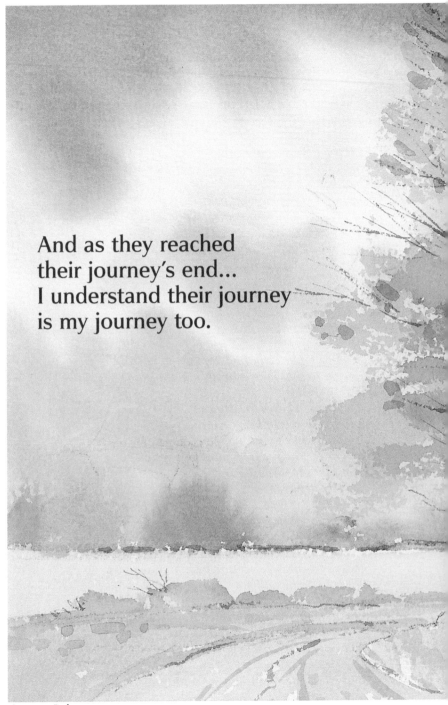

And as they reached
their journey's end...
I understand their journey
is my journey too.

Autumn Lake

Watercolour

"So the two women went on
until they came to Bethlehem."

Ruth 1:19

Love is creative. The word 'love' is never used in the story of Ruth yet its
threads weave in and out of the narrative and hold it all together. And
hold the two women together. How else would Naomi have so endeared
herself to her daughter-in-law that Ruth was willing to give up country
and culture to journey to Bethlehem? There was no star in the east to
guide her – it would have been in the west anyway for their journey – and
no prophecies to be read. Ruth made her pilgrimage for love.

The dynamic of Naomi's love created love in Ruth. Not as an
insubstantial echo, quickly fading, but with a solid permanence. "All you
need is love" sang the Beatles and I remember the impression they made
first time round in the 1960s. But they followed it up with another hit
"Can't buy me love." Self evident truths that most of us find out pretty
quickly in life.

Love is a wild flower. It propagates itself. Sows its own seed, extends its
own roots and blossoms into fruition almost at random, accidentally.
And like a seedling pushing up between stones it has a formidable power
of its own. It can't be created by deliberate choice. Naomi couldn't make
Ruth love her but love was created through a close and understanding
relationship arising out of shared sorrow. There's a circular dynamic to it.
Such a relationship creates love which strengthens relationship which
deepens love.

Yet love didn't solve all their problems. Philip Yancey says, "God does
not so much overrule as underrule."* On their return to Judah the two
women faced poverty and Naomi, judging by her outburst and bitterness
with her circumstances, was on the edge of depression. But something
brought her through it and, although it doesn't say so, I suggest that it
was the loving and faithful presence of Ruth, the asylum seeker.

*Reaching for the Invisible God by Philip Yancey, published by Zondervan
Publishing House 2000

Love makes the world go round,
that's what the cliché says.
I wonder, Lord.
Sometimes it seems the opposite is true.
It's greed and hate and violence
that call the shots,
and love is laughed at
as a game for idle moments,
a one-night stand,
never to be taken seriously.
And yet it never disappears.
Through all the suffering and loss
that life can bring
love springs anew
strong and persistent through the pruning.

Lord, I wish I could have walked
a mile or two with them,
and watched and listened
as they talked along the way.
I might have seen the sympathetic glances
in the tiredness as sunset loomed,
noticed the helping hand as footsteps faltered
underneath the loads they bore.
And though the word
is never mentioned in the story,
it was the oxygen of love
that motivated tired muscle and drove them on.

And as they reached their journey's end
– end or new beginning, Lord?
I think it's both –
I understand their journey is my journey too.
A pilgrimage that calls for love and constancy,
and faith to balance doubt,
never removed completely.
Then, as we pause for breath
and stretch our tired limbs,
I hear your laughter,
soft upon the wind.
And hear your voice.
It is accomplished.

"May the Lord repay you for what you have done."
Ruth 2:12

Boaz was a relative of Naomi, and a landowner. Naomi hoped that by sending her to work in his fields Ruth might strike up a relationship with him. Naomi's actions were an intriguing mixture of calculation, common sense and faith. The two women were living on the edge of survival and Naomi built on Ruth's willingness to go gleaning in the harvest fields. Only the poorest followed the harvesters and scrabbled for the stray ears of barley or wheat left lying in the dust. It was an ancient custom. The Jewish Law encouraged farmers to leave what had fallen for 'the poor and the alien' (Leviticus 19:9-10). Ruth qualified on both counts. Naomi had things carefully thought out, her strategy based on her knowledge of her people's traditions. In the tactics she instructed Ruth to use in approaching Boaz, she believed that he would act honourably without taking advantage.

Gossip must have been active as people exchanged news around the village well. Naomi's return would have caused comment, Ruth's arrival even more. Boaz must have heard too. He was impressed by what he'd heard and maybe he realised that he'd be expected to do something for his relatives, however distant. He saw Ruth in the fields and asked about her. Then when he knew who she was he spoke appreciatively of the way she'd cared for her mother-in-law. "May the Lord repay you for what you have done" he said (Ruth 2:12). From then on Naomi's plans ran just as she had hoped. Love and trust and obedience bring their reward, although not always as quickly or dramatically as in this case.

Perhaps we can learn from Naomi's planning. She had learned that crises must be faced and decisions made. Faith leads us to prayer and prayer leads us further into thought and action. Saying we'll pray about a problem is always good but it's sometimes a gesture of resignation. It can be the shrug of a shoulder, an implication that it's all we can do. That may be true and prayer is always worthwhile but I'm equally sure that God expects us to take the initiative when we can, to think situations through and use our common sense as well as our faith. One doesn't preclude the other.

"God helps those who help themselves" is a phrase often used selfishly but it's true in the sense of trying to find solutions to the problems that face us. That's not always possible of course but it may be more often than we're prepared to admit.

Through Naomi's careful and perceptive planning Ruth achieves new happiness and security in her husband and son, and Naomi finds joy and a future in her grandson. He in turn becomes the grandfather of King David and a whole chain of events begins which was to find fulfilment centuries later in Jesus. Ruth, the alien and asylum seeker, shows us that sharing in the kingdom of God has nothing to do with birth or race but everything to do with obedience and faith. Love opens the door to the kingdom without reserve. God rewards faith although the reward may be delayed. His purposes can take a long time to mature, but so does good wine. Neither can be hurried.

Lord, if I expected payment
for everything I do for you
I'd be a paid employee, not a friend,
and anyway if I were paid
on work accomplished
my earnings would be pretty small.
I'm glad to note
that's not the way your kingdom works.
In love's economy
the reward is in the doing
and washing feet
transforms a chore into a privilege.

Not that it's always easy, Lord,
I can't say that.
I'd like the comfort of acknowledgement at times,
to know my work's appreciated.
But in a sudden flash of truth
– hardly a revelation, Lord,
I should have seen it all the time –
I realise a little gratitude
for all you've done for me
would be appropriate.

And when I put that side by side
with what I've done for you
the balance doesn't balance anymore.
I'm deep in debt to you,
my life remortgaged in your favour,
a debt I cannot hope to meet,
not in a thousand years.

But, glory be, your love's a gift.
One that I don't deserve but willingly accept,
and if my life's response
is slower than you'd like
please give me time.
I may be slow
but I will walk the road as best I can.
With you.

I'm deep in debt to you,
my life remortgaged in your favour
a debt I cannot hope to meet,
not in a thousand years.

Morecambe Bay

Watercolour

Part Three

Into the Storm

Sea Mist, Norfolk

Watercolour

Reading – Mark 4:35-41

That day when evening came, he said to his disciples, "Let us go over to the other side." Leaving the crowd behind, they took him along, just as he was, in the boat. There were also other boats with him. A furious squall came up, and the waves broke over the boat, so that it was nearly swamped. Jesus was in the stern, sleeping on a cushion. The disciples woke him and said to him, "Teacher, don't you care if we drown?"

He got up, rebuked the wind and said to the waves, "Quiet! Be still!" Then the wind died down and it was completely calm.

He said to his disciples, "Why are you so afraid? Do you still have no faith?"

They were terrified and asked each other, "Who is this? Even the wind and the waves obey him!"

Imagine...

You are a disciple in the boat. The weather seems good. The sail flaps in the wind and bellies out in a sweet curve just above your head. Ropes sing, taut and vibrating. Listen to the splash and flow of water as the bow cuts its furrow through the lake. The air is damp, the breeze cool to the skin. The hum of voices from the shore diminishes, overlaid by these closer sounds.

It was a demanding crowd of people. It's good to get away from them, to be quiet together, to have time for your own thoughts. You can relax, stretch tired muscles. Feel the sweat begin to cool, the tension slowly ease from your neck and shoulders. Your legs feel heavy, your breathing slows. The world contracts, narrows to the boat and the people in it. You are part of an intimate circle of friends. It feels good. It's a serene moment, the day's work done. There's a sense of satisfaction and quiet wonder at what you've seen and heard with Jesus.

The light begins to fade. The gold on the horizon skims the tops of the ripples the boat creates. The hills begin to darken. Birds fly purposefully, heading home to roost. White gulls, black crows. In the stern of the boat Jesus shakes off his sandals, pulls a shawl round his shoulders and curls up on the old, stained cushion. You catch his glance. He smiles and closes his eyes. He is asleep.

Other fishing boats are following but there's an ominous change in the weather. The temperature drops, the wind freshens, spray from the boat's bow splashes higher, cold on the skin. You rouse yourself, look around, and as the heavy clouds gather you take in sail and huddle down as best you can. The noise increases as the sky darkens. The wind howls, ropes strain, the boat heaves, water breaks over the side, surges through the boat. You are wet and cold – and frightened. This is no ordinary storm. As it worsens the boat pitches, goes broadside on to the waves. You look at Jesus in the stern. He is still asleep.

Leaving the crowd behind...

Mark 4:36

It had been a long day. The crowd by the lake side had grown, pressing them down to the water's edge. A demanding crowd. There were village people, young and old, coming to hear this new teacher; lawyers, sceptical and superior, coming to confront yet another country preacher and tie him up in knots with their cold logic. Spies too, sent by the religious authorities to listen and report back. And always there were the sick and anxious, genuine in their need. The disciples had listened, learned and helped as Jesus had responded to all who came. Now it was evening and the sun was going down. The light was fading, blue to gold, silhouetting the hill tops round the lake. They'd accomplished a lot during the day but they'd only scratched the surface of the need. Now time had gone, their blood sugar levels were low, their energy used up. Whatever hadn't been done would just have to wait. They had to let go, to leave the rest for another day. Just like the end of our days.

Jesus recognised his disciples' need for quiet, the importance of leaving the crowd behind. People will take all that we can offer and often expect more than we can give. The feeling of being needed can be satisfying but it can be dangerous too – it massages the ego and can trap us into pride. Behind the words: "Nothing gets done if I'm not around" often lurks, "I need to feel needed." God never asks the impossible of us. If there really is no time to do something and if we really have little energy left then God doesn't expect it of us. Saying "no" may come hard but can be the right thing to say. Taking time out can be as important as the things we do. We aren't machines – and even machines do better with regular servicing otherwise they break down or wear out before they should.

It can be good to leave the crowd behind in another sense too. What the 'crowd' believes and approves often needs to be questioned. The standards society sets may not be the standards we should live by. Dumbing down isn't part of the Christian life. What the majority finds acceptable may not measure up to the ideal Jesus sets. I almost wrote moral majority there but that majority isn't always moral. The demands of the self-righteous, their unwillingness to allow freedom of choice to others, says more about a struggle for power than about love. Life without love isn't the sort of life Jesus offers. He asks us, expects us, to think for ourselves. He offers us true freedom to make our own decisions, informed and guided not by what the crowd calls for but by what love finds good and true. Jesus came to give us life, not drudgery.

Finally, let's note that the disciples left the crowd behind, not the other way round. The disciples were the explorers, moving forward to new ground. They, and we, are the pilgrims. You wouldn't always think so; sometimes we seem to use our faith more as a shelter than a stimulus, but Jesus calls us to leave the crowd and move forward, not to stand still. It may be risky and demanding but it gets our spiritual adrenalin going.

So often Lord
I am a hamster on a treadmill.
Going round and round incessantly
and getting nowhere.
At least the hamster can get off
and curl up in a corner of his cage,
but when he does
he finds he's back where he began,
no progress made.
I know the feeling.
Running to stand still, my energy burnt up.
And in the busyness no time for you.
I don't think that's your will for me –
for any of us, come to that.
Even you, Lord, rested on the Sabbath day.

Give me the grace to pause,
take breath
and reassess just where I am,
find time to hear your voice in quiet.
I know there's so much to be done
but earth will not implode
if I sit down and rest.
The pillars of the kingdom
won't come crashing down
if I let go my grip and stop.
And in the silence
as the treadmill of my mind stops turning
I'll hear you offering me
Shalom.
The peace that passes understanding.
And then refreshed,
my energy restored,
I can begin again to live
as you would have me live.

Still Waters

I know you'll show yourself
and still my storm
just when I need you most.

Watercolour

Jesus was in the stern, sleeping on a cushion.
Mark 4:38

It's a lovely, authentic touch of detail in the story and it's good to know that Galilean fishing boats had at least one cushion. Boat seats are hard; anyone who's spent a day fishing or taken a trip round the bay at any seaside resort knows that. And the disciples had had a busy day.

I picture the scene. A couple of disciples are getting the boat ready to sail. Jesus walks over, steps over the gunwale. A disciple takes his hand to steady him – wouldn't you like to have done that? – nods towards the stern and says, "Lord, you're tired. Take the cushion."

Another disciple hitches up his robe, wades into the water, pushes the boat out and clambers aboard. As they hoist the sail Jesus smiles at them, pulls his shawl around his shoulders, curls up on the cushion and closes his eyes. Was it a sleep of exhaustion, an indication of his humanity and vulnerability or was it a sleep of confidence in them? They were fishermen, some of them at least. They'd sailed boats on Galilee since childhood. Why should Jesus the carpenter get involved in the process? Whichever way you see the picture, Jesus leaves them to carry on.

The storm came with little warning. Storms often do. A few dark clouds, a sudden drop in temperature, the breeze quickening to gale force and suddenly they were lashed with rain. That's Galilee. The lake is surrounded by hills but in places there are deep valleys through which the wind can howl.

It must have been a powerful gale. They were experienced fishermen and knew what to do when storms came; take in sail, work the steering oar, keep the boat to the wind, but they were overwhelmed. Earlier in the story it says "there were also other boats with them". There's no mention of them anymore. In the gathering darkness they were alone and unable to cope. The waves rose, poured into the boat. Their clothes were soaked in cold water, heavy around their legs, impeding their movements. They bailed desperately – a waterlogged boat is unmanageable, dangerous. And they shouted above the noise of wind and wave.

"Jesus was in the stern, sleeping." That's what it says but I wonder about it. Was he really still asleep in the middle of all that noise? Gale force winds, waves slapping against the hull, water pouring in and the unpredictable heaving of the fishing boat. Or was he awake, lying there with his eyes shut, waiting to see how his friends would cope with the crisis? Whatever the truth, they thought he was asleep; thought that he was unconcerned about what was happening to them. It's an assumption easy to make when trouble comes. When we're battered by circumstance it often feels as though we're on our own and no one cares, not even God. But he is present, as Jesus was, and ready to waken when the time is right.

Lord, I've felt alone
so many times.
Bruised black and blue by life.
The tiles blown off the roof
of my self-confidence
by the storm.
The cold rain of doubt poured in,
flooding my faith.

I've cried to you
in desperation and uncertainty
and no one's answered.
I've thought you were asleep,
or far away, or even worse
that you'd abandoned me.
I'm sorry, Lord
but in the gathering darkness of my fears
clouds blackening my horizon
can so quickly blind me
to your presence.
The one thing I hang on to
each time the storm clouds gather,
is that you've graced my life
with mercy in the past
and so will come again to do the same.
Even there I've got it wrong.
How can you come again
when you're already here
whatever doubt may tempt me to assume?
Just help me face the wind
and wait.
I know you'll show yourself
and still my storm
just when I need you most.

The disciples woke him and said to him,
"Teacher, don't you care if we drown?"
Mark 4:38

Whether Jesus was still asleep or not, the disciples were wide awake, the adrenalin rushing through their veins., the storm inside each of them as powerful as that on the lake. They were more frightened than they'd ever been before in their lives. They'd done all they could, concentrated every bit of energy on the boat, but it didn't seem enough. They paused for breath and looked round. Suddenly they realised Jesus was still curled up in the stern of the boat, asleep. Their fear turned to anger. Fear and anger often go together; they can help us face physical danger and now the disciples' anger was directed at Jesus. He seemed unconcerned about the danger they were all in and oblivious to their struggle to survive. Their urgency made them say things they wouldn't usually say. One grabbed his shoulder, shook him awake, roughly. Another shouted above the wind – could it have been Peter? – "Don't you care if we drown?" Were they including Jesus in the we as well as themselves? When we read the story we already know the outcome but they were living through it in real time and didn't know how it would end. Their words were straight from the heart, uninhibited by tact or politeness.

Can we imagine anyone asking Jesus if he cared whether people lived or died? His life with them had been a witness to the sanctity in which he held all life, except perhaps his own. They'd experienced his concern for the sick in body, mind, and spirit; had seen his love for the poor and needy. Wasn't that enough to show the depth of his caring? But Jesus didn't rebuke them. He recognised their fear and responded.

"Don't you care if we drown?" People ask similar questions today when trouble strikes. Why does God let it happen? Why doesn't he do something about it? Blaming God is the easiest thing to do when problems come. To start with, it let's us off the hook. Many tragedies, large or small, are the result of human folly or greed: the greenhouse effect caused by pollution, landslides caused by the prodigal destruction of rainforest, the man next door thrown out of work by managers 'downsizing' their work force for extra profit. Events we could prevent. Whether Jesus is asleep or not is irrelevant. More apposite questions to ask might be "Are we asleep to tragedy?" "What are we doing to put things right?" Yet what about things we can't control? The earthquakes, the famines? The honest answer is that I don't know and neither does anyone else except the fundamentalist in every faith who says it's all

God's will. I don't believe it. To take that stance is to echo the disciples' question to Jesus and to accuse God of not caring whether we live or die. There simply – or not so simply – comes a point at which we have to stop looking for someone to blame and hang on in faith. There's no other way. That's what faith is for; to carry us through the bad bits when reason doesn't have an answer, and it can be hard.

The disciples saw a rapid and dramatic conclusion to their problem. Jesus stood up. His arms outstretched – whether to retain his balance or to command the storm we'll never know – and the storm is stilled. And in the sudden silence I can hear the disciples' laboured breathing, the trickle of water from their sodden clothes, almost hear the thudding of their hearts. Whatever they'd thought a few moments before, Jesus was awake and active in their lives. For us events aren't often as dramatic as that, although some testify to sudden drama in their lives. Most of us, most of the time, learn to live through the storms that come believing that Jesus is awake, is concerned and that one day the storm will change to calm.

Lord, when trouble comes
– and that's more often than I like
but less than many others have it
– I shout for you.
Hold out my hand
for you to kiss it better,
an infant in the nursery.
An instant fix is what I need,
something, someone,
to hold and keep me safe
in all eventualities.
Spiritual elastoplast to soothe the graze.
And when that doesn't happen,
and that's nearly all the time,
I wonder why.
I'm not complaining
– well, perhaps a little bit
– but are there moments when
you close your eyes on purpose
and offer me the chance to grow
by standing on my own two feet?
To grow in faith,
develop a maturity that strengthens me
and helps me look my problems in the face.
They're never easy, Lord,
those empty moments
when you let me think I'm on my own,
and I don't like them
any more than Peter and the others did,
but if it's what is best for me
I'll try to swallow it.
And if the storm continues
for longer than I think it should
help me remember
that you're in it with me
and that you haven't closed your eyes on me.
I know that's true.
It's simply that I like a little reassurance,
now and then.
Forgive me, Lord.

Towards the Bay, Morecambe, *Pastel*

> "He said to his disciples, "Why are you so afraid?
> Do you still have no faith?"
>
> Mark 4:40

In the sudden calm that followed the sudden storm the disciples' emotions were in chaos. I imagine them motionless, frozen in position, bewildered, looking at Jesus in wide-eyed wonder. Storms didn't end so abruptly and they certainly didn't end when someone told them to. They were on the edge of what they knew and understood, staring into something way beyond their experience. Of course they were afraid.

Fear is a reaction that tells us to run away or struggle, or do whatever will make us safe. It isn't always rational in its response and doesn't always produce the result we'd like. From narratives in the Bible we learn that fear seems to be an immediate human response to the presence of God – or of one of his messengers. Moses "hid his face, because he was afraid to look at God." (Exodus 3:6). And when the angel appeared to Mary and later to the shepherds in Bethlehem's fields, they were all afraid.

The story of the storm on Galilee seems to imply that fear and faith are opposites which can't be yoked together. Jesus' question, "Why are you so afraid? Do you still have no faith?" suggests that the one elbows out the other. That's fine for a sermon on Sunday morning but most people's life experience tells them that it's not as simple as that. We're human and we are afraid of many things. That's the way we're made. We often try to hide our fears, particularly in a Christian context, because we're afraid – and that's another fear – that our lack of faith will bring the disapproval of other believers. We pretend to a courage we don't possess and that arouses the guilt that leads to more fear.

Jesus can deal with it and he deals with it in love. As the writer of John's first letter tells us "perfect love drives out fear, because fear has to do with punishment." (1 John 4:18). When Jesus asks his disciples in the boat about their fear it isn't a confrontation we witness. I hear his voice, not strong and challenging as theirs had been when they woke him, but gentle and sympathetic. He'd seen their fear and responded to it. Now he helped them to understand that his presence could strengthen faith and that faith can, slowly perhaps, deal with their fear. And with the fears that many of us face daily.

"Why are you so afraid? Jesus asked. Fear lessens as faith grows, but in an imperfect world full of imperfect people, and an imperfect church full of imperfect Christians, we stand with the disciples. I'm not sure that our love and faith can ever be strong or complete enough to drive out fear totally. In my experience faith isn't the same as certainty. Certainty doesn't need faith. I'm certain that two plus two equals four. That's a fact and I don't need faith to accept it. Faith is what I cling to when doubt and fear try to take over my life and, in a disturbing but comforting way, faith and doubt go together.

Faith isn't the conquering of all doubt and fear. It's the courage to believe in the midst of it. There are folk who never appear to doubt and who feel no need to ask difficult questions of life. In one way that may be a blessing but in another way asking questions and facing doubts can lead us into new truth – or a deeper understanding of the truth we already hold. And it's through the truth that followers of the way can find new life. Which is what Jesus was and is and offers us.

I've been afraid, Lord, many times,
you're well aware of that.
Yes, I believe in you,
in goodness and in love.
In truth,
although that's not an easy one
when I have to face myself
and, more, face you.
In truth, I am afraid of many things.
The calm and cool exterior
I try so hard to show
can sometimes mask a multitude of doubts.
An avalanche of questions
roaring down into my life
which threatens to engulf
and freeze my faith.
Questions borne out of insecurity
to which the pulpit words of preachers offer little.
I'm only human.
Very human, that you know.

I'm sure you don't object to questioning.
My mind is your creation
and I can't be blamed for using it.
Yet questions aren't always answered
in a way I understand.
And faith, I'm sure,
is not the conquering of fear and doubt
but more the courage to believe
within my doubt and fear.
The comfort is
that when I come to you for strength
in fear and trembling
I find your hand stretched out for mine.
And in the storm-free silence
I can hear your patient reassurance
telling me
that hand in hand with you
I can survive and grow,
and leave the answers for another day.

They were terrified and asked each other, "Who is this?
Even the wind and the waves obey him!"

Mark 4:41

The end of the storm didn't resolve the crisis for the disciples. They were desperately afraid then but once it was over their fear grew. They were terrified. They couldn't get to grips with the power Jesus had exercised. They'd recognised his authority as a teacher – that's what had drawn them to him in the first place. They'd seen and accepted his healing powers, but this was different. They were out of their depth. No one had ever shown this sort of power over nature and it frightened them beyond anything the gale had done. The peace after the storm brought them no peace and they began to ask each other, "Who is this?"

I notice that they ask each other, not Jesus. The conversation, if you can call it that, had been with Jesus. Their fear had made them bold but this development was so shattering that they no longer had the courage to speak to him directly. Instead they asked each other, "Who is this Jesus?" An inspired teacher, a gifted healer, a charismatic leader? One minute he was a human being like them, tired and asleep in the boat. The next he was using a power no one had ever used before. Even though they lived so closely with Jesus their understanding grew only slowly. It was much later in Caesarea Philippi that Peter eventually blurted out the truth that Jesus was the Christ, the promised Messiah. And even then their understanding was incomplete.

Jesus was patient with them. He didn't bully them or push them harder than they were able to respond. He treated them with what Mother Julian of Norwich, a Christian mystic writing in the 14th century, called 'his exquisite courtesy'. * And that's how he treats us today, at least in my experience. The revelation of his true nature may hit some people with dramatic suddenness but for most of us it comes a little at a time. As we travel the road with him Jesus gradually draws us into a progressively deeper appreciation of who he is.

It can be an awesome experience – who are we to penetrate fully into the mystery of Jesus? – but we are offered the opportunity to draw nearer to him, to enter more deeply into his life. The question never fully leaves us and it is never fully answered. The great thing is that the longer we travel with him the question matters less . We know all we need to know.

* *Enfolded in Love. Daily Readings with Julian of Norwich. Darton, Longman and Todd. ©1980 The Julian Shrine.*

Lord, you are my friend,
my companion on the way.
The one who gives me strength
to face the storms you do not choose to calm.
My comforter on cold and cloudy days
who warms my life with love.
Yet ever contrary and still in love,
the one who wakes me up, pushes me on,
challenges me a little at a time
to take the world just as it comes.
(A confrontation I would still avoid if you would let me.)

But in the warmth of friendship
let me never take you lightly
or undervalue what you've done,
are doing yet, for me.
Your presence with me is an awesome thing,
or would be
if I realised more fully what it means.
I find it almost frightening as they did, Lord,
That you, creator God,
should share my life,
should share your life with me,
should walk with me
as though I really mattered.
And that in loving revelation
you should be willing,
oh so patiently,
to show me who you are.

My mind can't comprehend your nature
but I hold with reverence
the little understanding that I have
and wait for more to be revealed
in your good time.

...they took him along, just as he was, in the boat.

The disciples took Jesus just as he was. At first reading the words describe an ordinary everyday event. Jesus was tired and so were they. They'd had a busy and demanding day dealing with the needs of the people around them. We know the feeling. They'd had no time to eat or change their clothes and relax. Now they needed to get away from the crowd and that's what they did.

With a little thought the words take on a deeper resonance. Taking Jesus just as he is suggests the need for a wholehearted acceptance of him, of who he is (the disciples had had problems with that in the aftermath of the storm), and of his teaching. It's so easy to commit ourselves to him in moments of deep emotion but so hard to live out that response in the stress of daily life. Can we accept the whole range of Jesus' teaching? Can we live out the bits which challenge us and make us deeply uneasy? We're all for love when love paints a gentle stress-free picture of life, but what about the self-denial, the demands for forgiveness? That's all part of the love that Jesus showed and taught, and a major part.

There's an ancient Greek legend about a giant named Procrustes. He lived in a castle beside a busy road. Each evening he would invite a passing pilgrim to share his hospitality for the night but it wasn't what the pilgrim expected. Procrustes had a bed for his guests. If the guest was too tall for the bed the giant would cut off the pilgrim's legs. If he was too short for the bed he'd be put on the rack and lengthened. In each case the unfortunate traveller was made to fit the bed perfectly but I imagine it didn't really help him. We can do something similar with our faith if we're not careful. It's tempting to try to shape God in our own image, to take Jesus' teaching and cut and rearrange it to fit into the pattern of our own ideas. It doesn't work. We are invited to take Jesus just as he is.

After all, that's the way God accepts each one of us. That's the wonder of his love and it demands a great deal of his forbearance. And if God accepts me just as I am then it suggests very strongly that I need to accept other people in a similar way. It's easy to want to change others, our family and friends – out of love of course – rather than accept them with all their faults. Maybe we would like them to be a bit different but it has to be God who initiates the change in them. When we try it can quickly become a power struggle, and power and love have little in common.

Finally, I see the whole story of the storm on the lake as a simple metaphor for the Christian life, a living parable. We step into the boat of faith with Jesus, to travel with him, to take risks, to journey with him into an uncharted future. It may not be a physical journey. We may live in the same house for 20 years, attend the same church all our lives but life with Jesus is an exploration, an adventure that never ends. It takes courage to accept him just as he is, committing ourselves to him without conditions. The storms we encounter may not be stilled with the same speed as was the disciples' storm. We may have to learn to live with ours but he will be in them with us, even though we may think at times that he's asleep!

Mother Julian, whom I quoted earlier, wrote: He did not say, "You shall not be tempest-tossed, you shall not be work-weary, you shall not be discomforted." But he said, "You shall not be overcome." *

And another Christian, Jeremy Taylor, writing in the 17th century, said "We are far safer in the middle of the storm with God, than anywhere else without him."

Enfolded in Love. Daily Readings with Julian of Norwich, Darton, Longman & Todd. ©1980 The Julian Shrine

Just as you are, Lord?
I know that's what it says
but there's a difference –
I've always got a but –
the difference is
you're you, I'm me.
And that puts such a gulf between us,
so difficult to leap.
There have been times
I thought I could be good enough for you,
might bridge the gap
if only I could try a little harder.
That if I made another effort
I could generate the virtue
that would make me more acceptable to you.
But always there's a leak in my resolve.
It drains away and leaves me high and dry.
Nothing accomplished, no progress made
and lurking in the background of my mind
the question 'Was it worth the effort?'

Then as I pause
and ask 'What next?'
I realise what in my heart I'd always known.
That if I take you as you are
I find that you've already done the same for me.
There are no spiritual exams to pass,
no grades to gain.

And as the truth hits home
the burden falls away,
like Pilgrim's in the story.
You're in my life already.
The very longing that I feel
says that you're here with me
and all the deep desire of my heart's
a simple mirror image of your love for me.
Then all I need to do
Is look at my relationships in this new light.

I'll need to think that through.
Just give me time.
I'm glad that you're a patient God.

The very longing that I feel
says that you're here with me
and all the deep desire of my heart's
a simple mirror image
of your love for me.

A.B.ASKEW

Sea Mist, Norfolk

Watercolour

Part Four

Through Samaria

Blue Hills, Cumbria

Watercolour

Reading - John 4:4-30

Now Jesus had to go through Samaria. So he came to a town in Samaria called Sychar, near the plot of ground Jacob had given to his son Joseph. Jacob's well was there, and Jesus, tired as he was from the journey, sat down by the well. It was about the sixth hour.

When a Samaritan woman came to draw water, Jesus said to her, "Will you give me a drink?" (His disciples had gone into the town to buy food.) The Samaritan woman said to him, "You are a Jew and I am a Samaritan woman. How can you ask me for a drink?" (For Jews do not associate with Samaritans.) Jesus answered her, "If you knew the gift of God and who it is that asks you for a drink, you would have asked him and he would have given you living water."

"Sir, " the woman said, "you have nothing to draw with and the well is deep. Where can you get this living water? Are you greater than our father Jacob, who gave us the well and drank from it himself, as did also his sons and his flocks and herds?" Jesus answered, "Everyone who drinks this water will be thirsty again, but whoever drinks the water I give him will never thirst. Indeed, the water I give him will become in him a spring of water welling up to eternal life." The woman said to him, "Sir, give me this water so that I won't get thirsty and have to keep coming here to draw water."

He told her, "Go, call your husband and come back." "I have no husband," she replied. Jesus said to her, "You are right when you say you have no husband. The fact is, you have had five husbands, and the man you now have is not your husband, What you have just said is quite true." "Sir," the woman said, "I can see that you are a prophet. Our fathers worshipped on this mountain, but you Jews claim that the place where we must worship is in Jerusalem." Jesus declared, "Believe me, woman, a time is coming when you will worship the Father neither on this mountain nor in Jerusalem. You Samaritans worship what you do not know; we worship what we do know, for salvation is from the Jews. Yet a time is coming and has now come when the true worshippers will worship the Father in spirit and truth, for they are the kind of worshippers the Father seeks. God is spirit, and his worshippers must worship in spirit and in truth."

The woman said, "I know that Messiah" (called Christ) "is coming. When he comes, he will explain everything to us." Then Jesus declared, "I who speak to you am he." Just then his disciples returned and were surprised to find him talking with a woman. But no one asked, "What do you want?" Or, "Why are you talking with her?" Then, leaving her water jar, the woman went back to the town and said to the people, "Come, see a man who told me everything I ever did. Could this be the Christ?" They came out of the town and made their way towards him.

Reading – John 4:39-42

Many of the Samaritans from that town believed in him because of the woman's testimony, "He told me everything I ever did." So when the Samaritans came to him, they urged him to stay with them, and he stayed two days. And because of his words many more became believers. They said to the woman, "We no longer believe just because of what you said; now we have heard for ourselves, and we know that this man really is the Saviour of the world."

Imagine...

It's midday. The sun is hot, the road is rough and dusty, rutted with cart tracks. Jesus and his disciples have walked since early morning. It's the second day of their journey through the hill country – Sychar is nearly 40 miles from Jerusalem – and as they turn a corner they see ahead of them the cluster of flat-roofed houses which is the village. The disciples are apprehensive. Samaria doesn't welcome Jews. There's a long history of conflict between the two communities. They don't know why Jesus has chosen to come this way and they walk together as a group, keeping close to him. No one lags behind.

They reach the well on the edge of the village and pause. They put down the bundles they carry, take deep breaths and stretch. Their clothes stick to their backs in the heat. They're hungry and Jesus tells them to go and buy food. The disciples hesitate, exchange glances. They're reluctant to buy Samaritan food. It would make them ritually unclean, but Jesus' instruction and their hunger overcome their prejudices and they set off.

Jesus is left alone. He breathes in deeply, sighs and looks around, then sits on the low stone wall that surrounds the well. He leans back, enjoys the moment and begins to relax. Then he peers down the shaft of the well, takes in the cool damp smell. The well is deep and dark. There's just a glimmer of light, a round reflection of sky and his face shimmering on the surface of the water. He picks up a pebble and drops it down the well. There's a pause and then a satisfying plop and an echo as the stone splashes into the water.

Distant sounds come from the village. Dogs barking, a murmur of voices, the sound of a blacksmith's hammer. Nearby a bird sings, then stops. There's movement on the road. A woman walking, a clay water pot cradled in her elbow, its weight on her hip. In her other hand she carries a coiled rope and a leather bucket. She approaches the well and looks sideways at Jesus, not making eye contact with the stranger. There's a pause. Then Jesus speaks. "Will you give me a drink?"

Now Jesus had to go through Samaria.

John 4:4

The air was still and Jesus was enjoying a few valued moments of quiet at the well. The disciples had disappeared down the road, passing without comment the lone woman carrying her water pot. There was no one else in sight. It was a moment to relax.

The Pharisees had been stirring up opposition to Jesus in and around Jerusalem and now he was heading back to Galilee. The story tells us that Jesus had to go through Samaria to get there. That wasn't literally true. It was certainly the shortest, most direct route but there was another and it was the alternative most Jews took to avoid trouble. Jews and Samaritans disliked each other. Their enmity went back centuries and, rather than risk harassment, Jews bypassed Samaria. They went a longer way – east from Jerusalem over the River Jordan and north up the valley until they could re-cross the river back into Galilean territory, avoiding Samaria altogether. It was tedious but safer.

The pressure on Jesus to go through Samaria had nothing to do with geography. It was some inner compulsion that drove him to take the less conventional route – when was Jesus ever conventional?– at the prompting of the Spirit. It must have surprised the disciples; another unexpected journey for them.

Three explosive, emotional reasons had created the tension between Jew and Samaritan. Matters of religion, race and sex. Mercifully there were no tabloid newspapers to exploit the situation and make it even worse. Simplifying the problem, Samaritans had a Jewish background but differed strongly about the scriptures. They also disagreed about where to worship. They had their own temple on Mount Gerazim until Jews destroyed it in about 128 BC. Memories were long and the Samaritans still resented it.

Centuries ago the Assyrians had conquered the land and the Samaritans had collaborated with them and intermarried with the invaders. What should have been a matter of ancient history with little relevance to the day was still a live issue. To the Jews this intermingling made Samaritans 'unclean'. And that of course had added a strong element of sex to it all. A whole group of people condemned *en masse* not for what they'd done but for who they were seen to be. They were blamed for a history they'd inherited but for which they weren't responsible.

It's a story of prejudice with a contemporary ring for us. None of us is immune to prejudice, much of it unconscious. We're quick to judge, to take sides, and to grab the flimsiest of reasons to exclude people. Wearing the wrong clothes, living in the wrong country, even the wrong part of town, speaking with the wrong accent is enough. Writing a few years later, St Paul gloried in the truth that "there is neither Jew nor Greek, slave nor free, male nor female, for you are all one in Christ Jesus." (Galatians 3:28). A truth sometimes honoured more in word than action.

We exclude people, God forgive us, through the way we worship, in the way we interpret scripture, even questioning the place of women in the church. And it's so easy to try to justify it as God's will rather than identify it as human frailty. That didn't work for Jesus. The lowly and despised were to be honoured in the kingdom he proclaimed, and they would include Samaritans – something he would make clear as he talked with the woman who was now coming to the well.

Lord, I go reluctantly
through Samaria,
as I suspect the disciples did.
My own Samaria.
There's territory in my life I won't explore,
places and issues I don't want to think about,
people I want no contact with.
It's easier to turn my back and whistle,
pretend that they're not there.
I am unwilling
to wander through the wilderness
of my own prejudice,
confront the unnamed fears and insecurity
that feed and grow on ignorance
and lead me to condemn and spurn
people and things that I don't know.

Yet as I walk with you
maybe I'll find the courage and the honesty
to face those unacknowledged fears,
to see them as they are,
and one day learn to love
all those who turn me off.
And as I recognise the worth
of those I had discounted,
I'll realise I stand with them in need of you.
Then, stretching out my understanding
and my hand,
I'll find another hand
stretched out to me.
I thank you, Lord,
that prejudice
has never stopped you reaching out
to touch and bless,
and heal the crying corners of my life.
And then in one astounding burst
of real humility
(protect me Lord from being proud of it,
it doesn't happen very often!)
I'll realise that I, not they,
stand most in need of your forgiveness.

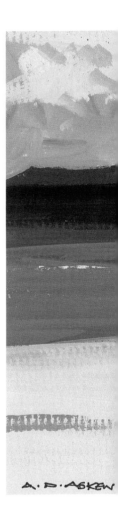

A. D. ASKEW

Bright Day, Isle of Mull   *Gouache*

> When a Samaritan woman came to draw water, Jesus said to her,
> "Will you give me a drink?"
>
> John 4:7

A friend challenged me to take a long look at the Samaritan woman and to see her as a real human being. It's not easy to drop the assumptions of a lifetime but it's worth trying. Usually, as we read of Jesus' encounter with her, we concentrate on his words and she remains a cardboard cut-out, a foil, the person who makes the conversation possible and nothing more.

I wish I knew her name. It's so impersonal to keep calling her 'the woman' or 'she' but there's nothing else we can do. She comes into the picture preoccupied with her own troubles. Life hasn't been good to her. She's carrying burdens, not just a bucket. She's had difficulties with relationships, particularly with men. Sometimes there'd been a wedding ceremony, at other times not. That's according to Jesus' words later on, and she never denied them. Why so many problems? The easiest and simplest answer is to dismiss her as immoral, a woman who despised convention and went wherever her emotions led her. In other words to blame her. But that's too facile, quick judgements often are. Prejudice is a weed with deep roots.

I wonder about her early life, her childhood. Had she been ill-treated, abused in ways that made it impossible for her to trust people? She'd had difficulties building stable relationships. She was a damaged personality, a woman constantly looking for love and affirmation but always looking in the wrong place with the wrong men. She began each new relationship with the hope that it would be better and more loving than the last but she was always disappointed. She would blame herself for her failures, each time losing a little more self-esteem, her personality if not her body bruised and battered by her latest encounter.

Why did she come to the well at noon? Women – and it was usually the women who did the heavy work of carrying water – chose to come in the cool of the morning or late afternoon rather than in the heat of midday. As they drew water they exchanged news. There was talk of the weather, the harvest, the latest marriages, births and deaths. I wonder, was she ostracised, excluded by a combination of her history and the self-righteousness of people whose faults were less obvious, more carefully hidden? We don't know but imagination makes her a flesh-and-blood person and perhaps one as much sinned against as sinning.

As she neared the well where Jesus sat their eyes met briefly before she looked away. There was a moment's silence while Jesus continued to look at her. Then he spoke. "Will you give me a drink?" She was surprised. Her defences went up. She'd had enough to put up with from the townsfolk without being approached by strange men. This was wrong, a shocking thing to do. The well was a public place, anyone might be watching. Men didn't speak to women they didn't know and her response could easily be misunderstood. The best defence was attack and she challenged him with society's conventions. If he took a drink from her he'd become ritually unclean. Was that really what he wanted or was there another hidden agenda to his request? She was sceptical, unsure, suspicious.

Jesus was thirsty. Was it as simple as that? The one who'd endured 40 days in the desert, who'd turned water into wine, showing his humanity by asking for a drink of water? Or had Jesus read the woman's character and her need as she approached the well, and asked for a drink simply to begin a conversation with her? A conversation most people would have avoided. Society's rules may have dictated one thing but the compassion at the heart of Jesus always provoked him into breaking them when it seemed the better alternative. And in doing so he set the scene for the beginning of a new relationship which would heal the wounds of her earlier experiences, transcend her distrust and doubt, draw her into faith and transform her life.

I wish I knew her name, Lord,
the woman at the well.
She walks into my life
nameless,
burdened by a history
I shall never know.
Searching for love
in ways and places I shall never visit,
stubbing her toes on broken hopes
that cluttered the corners of her life,
just so much rubbish no one wants.

And always disappointed, Lord,
until you came into her life.
And into mine.
Disturbing with a love
that digs up secrets,
unlocks the truths
I'd rather not remember.
Challenging me
to face my failures.
Helping each one of us
to look in honesty
at what we were without you
and to show us
what we can become with you.

Our deepest selves.
Your judgement's only to restore
and offer us a new beginning.
And as she found in you
the love she'd searched for all her life,
in greater depth than she could ever hope to find,
so too may we.
I wish I knew her name, Lord,
but I can rest content
in knowing that she's known by you,
enfolded in your love for all eternity.
And knowing that her name
is written in your book of life,
next, I believe, to mine.
Thanks be to God.

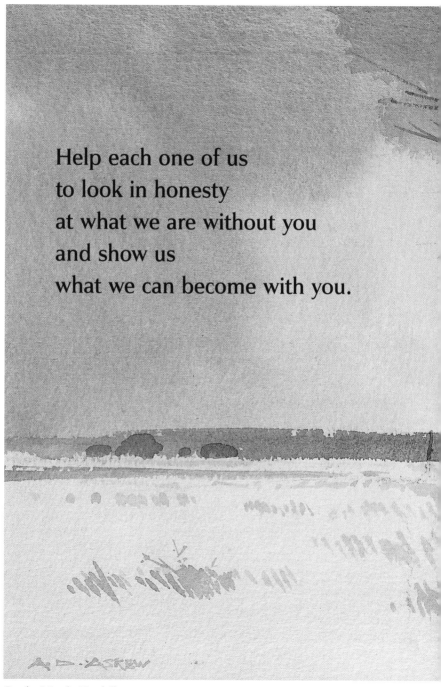

Help each one of us
to look in honesty
at what we are without you
and show us
what we can become with you.

On the Marsh, Norfolk

Watercolour

Jesus answered her, "If you knew the gift of God
and who it is that asks you for a drink,
you would have asked him
and he would have given you living water."

John 4:10

Promises, promises, she'd heard it all before. There was a splash as the woman threw her bucket down the well. She began to pull on the rope hand over hand, gasping with the effort. The bucket was heavy. She looked sideways at Jesus. She was wary, unsure, questioning. Men had offered her many things, made many promises, but they'd all come to nothing. She wondered what Jesus really wanted, what was hiding behind his words. He had no bucket, the well was deep. Her response was another question – how could he give her living water?

Living water. That was what all well-diggers hoped for, prayed for. Not a still or stagnant pond but a flowing stream, constantly replenishing itself. After the labour of sinking a well 50, 100 feet deep, they hoped to find a stream of water that never dried up and could be relied on throughout the year. Tradition said that the Samaritans' ancestor, Jacob, had dug this well centuries before and that his sons and flocks and herds had drunk from it. I assume his daughters had too, although they're not mentioned in the story even though they certainly drew the water for the family! And as she swung the bucket of water over the lip of the well and poured the water into her jar, the woman challenged Jesus. "Can you do better than Jacob?"

Jesus waited as she lowered her bucket into the well again, then began to clarify the point of the conversation. "I'm not talking about the water you're splashing around. You'll be back here tomorrow and the next day for more of that," he said and went on to offer her something quite different – eternal life. The timeless life of God himself, ever renewing, inexhaustible living water. In the next chapter of his gospel John records Jesus' words, "Whoever hears my word and believes him who has sent me has eternal life and will not be condemned; he has crossed over from death to life." (John 5:24) That's all in the present tense, a reality that can be grasped now, not just in the future. A greater promise than any the woman had been offered by anyone in the past. A new life beginning here and now. As she moved from one failing relationship to the next, the woman must have yearned for something better, some quality of life she'd never known. This was it.

She paused as she drew up the heavy bucket a second time. The conversation was getting too deep for her, deeper than the well. It was hard to keep it under control. She tried to hide behind a little sarcasm, "Great," she said, "I'd like some of that. It'd save me having to come back here every day," and maybe adding under her breath, "and having to listen to the sort of nonsense you're talking."

There's a paradox here though. "Whoever drinks the water I give him will never thirst," said Jesus (John 4:14). But we do thirst. Once we've tasted the richness he brings we constantly thirst for more, we can never get enough. The more we experience of God, the more we desire. The thirst is unquenchable. But this is a different thirst. It's a thirst for fulfilment which can turn the sterility of our personal desert into fruitfulness.

Jesus decided it was time to cut through all the verbal fencing. "Fetch your husband," he said. I don't know why he asked her to call her husband, and we're not told if her partner actually came, but there was a moment's silence. It was broken by the sound of water as she filled her jar, playing for time. She mumbled, "I have no husband." "I know," said Jesus. I don't know how he knew, what clues he'd picked up from the way she dressed, or the body language as she walked to the well at midday and talked with him. However it happened his words deflated her, burst any bubble of pretence she'd been hiding behind.

We need to pause now to listen sensitively for the tone of voice as Jesus spoke. I believe he said those words quietly, lovingly. There was no harshness, nothing judgmental in what he said. He spoke, not to condemn her but to start her gently on the road of awareness and self-examination that would awaken her to her need. A journey beginning where she was, with all her fears, disappointments and longings, and leading to a fulfilment beyond any dreams she had left. A journey we all have to make as we begin to see ourselves as God sees us and to grasp the offer of change and transformation which he holds out.

A cup of water for forgiveness?
A fair exchange I call it, Lord,
although I don't know
if you ever got the drink you asked her for.
It was an offer no one could refuse.
I nearly said 'A bargain'
but if there's one thing that I've learned
it's that there is no bargaining with you.
There is no fair exchange
because what little I can offer
is far outweighed
by what you give.
The giving's all from you,
the taking mine.

Sometimes I question,
and repeat the worldly wisdom
that if an offer
seems too good for truth,
it really is.
That there's a catch,
small print I haven't read,
the weasel clauses carefully thought out
to put me at a disadvantage.
There often is but not this time.
The promises you make are real,
and true and lasting.
Promises beyond my wildest dreams,
starting today.
Promises of life
drawn from a well of love
your sacrifice has dug,
tapping a living stream
that waters and enriches
all I am and do.
And all you ask of me is that I drink,
and drink again.
My thirst is ever quenched –
and never quenched in you –
because the more I have of you
the more I want.
I'll throw my bucket in again.

> "Sir," the woman said, "I can see that you are a prophet.
> Our fathers worshipped on this mountain,
> but you Jews claim that the place
> where we must worship is in Jerusalem."
>
> John 4:19-20

When we're embarrassed we try to change the subject; lead the conversation in a more comfortable direction. That's what the Samaritan woman was trying to do. She hoped to divert Jesus' attention away from her personal life by trying to flatter him. She called him a prophet. Perhaps there was just a trace of irony in her words. She'd been very much on the defensive so far and sarcasm is a useful weapon when you're losing the argument.

She followed up by baiting him with a theological question that was a living issue for both Jews and Samaritans. "Where should believers worship? Here in Samaria or in Jerusalem?" A question with a dangerous history and crucial to the differences between the two communities. Surely this would divert Jesus' attention.

It didn't. He wasn't caught out. He used the question to focus on the truth about worship, a truth that would resolve the whole issue. The place, he said, doesn't matter. God is spirit, free-flowing like the living water Jesus was offering the woman, and worship – our intimacy with God – is a spirit-filled life. It's a pure heart that counts, insofar as flawed human beings are capable of it, and not clean clothing or choosing the right place. True worship isn't connected in any way with race or nation, has little to do with tradition or ritual, but everything to do with the sincerity and commitment with which we seek God. And, to bring it up to date, has nothing to do with the particular brand of Christian worship our diverse personalities favour.

And before we get carried away in an attempt to define true worship and end up proclaiming that it is of course the particular way we do things, let's remember that the only judge of the sincerity with which we offer ourselves to God is God himself. It can be hard disentangling the *spirit* of worship from the *habit* of worship because habit can be so strong. Jesus' words offer us a loving freedom, a chance to break the chains that constrain us – 'breaking the tyranny of normality' as someone memorably put it. It takes courage to step over the boundaries we set and enter into the freedom God offers, but he invites us, challenges us to do it.

Jesus' answer wasn't what she'd been expecting. God's answers rarely are. She struggled with the thought, then gave up. With a shrug she distanced herself from the discussion which she'd started. "Oh well," she said, "when Messiah comes he'll explain it all." It's so easy to shrug off responsibility, to leave the hard-thinking and decision-making to others – that's the way cults begin – but that's not what life asks of us, nor what God asks of us. Suddenly, startlingly, Jesus crystallised the whole conversation. "When Messiah comes," she'd said. "That's me," replied Jesus. If she was still holding her bucket at this moment she would have dropped it. And, incidentally, in saying this Jesus answered her earlier question about whether he was greater than her ancestor Jacob. He was. Then, before she could recover, the disciples returned and the conversation came to a sudden end.

What a pity. I want the conversation to continue. I want to see the shock on her face, her incomprehension turn into certainty as Jesus explains. I want to see her defensiveness turn into the radiance of knowing that she is in the presence of God's son. To see her open her life to the promise of this man she's met by the well, a promise that would be fulfilled and would never disappoint her. An assurance that would send her back to her people full of wonder and with an urge to share what she's discovered with them. But the disciples return and we are brought down to earth.

She has no name, Lord,
I'm coming back to that same thought again.
It's not exactly true of course.
She had a name,
it's just that we don't know it.
She had a name as everybody has,
a name given at birth
or shortly after.
Chosen with care and lovingly
to mirror all the hopes
her parents had for her.
A name shortened in affection
and used to place her in the family,
give her identity and value.

Then as she grew into a woman
and her relationships went wrong,
I'm sure that people
called her other names,
and not so complimentary.
Names called, not out of love
but in harsh criticism
of the way of life she'd chosen –
or had forced on her, I don't know which.

Lord, guard me from the same mistake
of making judgement,
lightly entered into,
not knowing all the facts.
Of blaming folk
for faults and failings not their own.
Open my eyes to see in others
all the possibilities you saw in her
and offer what I can
to build new life in them.

Then Jesus declared, "I who speak to you am he."
Just then his disciples returned
and were surprised to find him talking to a woman.

John 4:26-27

When I began this study I felt that the woman's sudden return to town, leaving her water jar at the well, was the result of the disciples' return. It was one thing being alone with Jesus but the sudden presence of a whole group of men disturbed her. They made no comment about Jesus talking with her but I'm sure they'd make their disapproval clear. A raised eyebrow, a cool stare, the corners of the mouth turned down. It's easy to freeze someone out without saying a word.

Now though, I feel it was something else that moved her. A sudden surge of joy, the living water bubbling up into her life, only half understood but real. A need to go back and share her experience with others, even those who had used her so badly. In a way she was travelling through her own Samaria, confronting the prejudice of people who'd deeply humiliated her. She was ready to face and conquer her own resentment towards them and thought only of sharing her experience. "Come, see a man who told me everything I ever did. Could this be the Christ?" she asked. I hear longing in her voice. A yearning that Jesus was truly who he claimed to be. Someone who would keep his promises and turn her life around.

"Everything I ever did." In Christ's presence, in the sudden opening of her eyes, her life flashed through her mind and she saw herself with a greater clarity and truth than ever before. She was reborn. The more I read this story the more I place it beside that of the parable of the prodigal son. Not just because it helps the gender balance but because both stories encapsulate the essence of the Christian message – the recognition of human weakness and vulnerability, and the possibility of an individual life being turned around and renewed through God's loving forgiveness and acceptance. It's so easy to give up on people. Jesus didn't.

Perhaps the most significant thing in this episode at the well is that this was the first time Jesus openly said that he was the Messiah, and he said it to a woman who was a Samaritan. Racism has no place in his kingdom. It's open to all and while it's not said in words, Jesus accepted her as she was. Her past, blameworthy or not, erased. Her dignity restored. Accepted as part of the new community Jesus was creating. The barriers of race, gender and prejudice torn down, her welcome into the kingdom immediate and unconditional.

She responded by sharing her new life and became the first woman evangelist of the Christian church. The purpose of the journey, so unexpected by the disciples, completed. As her new life began, did all her earlier problems suddenly disappear? We're not told but I doubt it. That's hardly the way life works. Faith doesn't always sweep away our difficulties. Yet we can be sure of one thing – that in Christ she found a new focus for living, new values that helped her see her situation in a new way and respond to it in his strength.

In clothing this conversation between Jesus and the Samaritan woman with my imagination I've been disturbed by her anonymity. Our lives are shaped by so many influences – our parents, families and friends – but fashioned too by people we shall never know or name. Brief contacts with folk who came into our lives, helped and went on their way. Faces we can recall only dimly. People we never met at all but whose teaching and work have altered the way we think and act, and have enriched our lives, the crowd of witnesses whose names only God knows.

Finally though, we're told that Jesus stayed with the Samaritans for two days. I love to imagine him staying in the woman's home – he was comfortable staying with the despised and rejected – and meeting her partner and her children.

And learning her name for himself.

You gave your disciples a hard time, Lord,
as they tried to come to terms
with who you were
and how you lived your life.
I don't know their reaction
as they saw the two of you together,
you and the woman.
It wasn't done.
The rules and regulations of society forbade it.
And I can guess their disapproval.
I've seen it many times in church
when someone steps across
the invisible boundaries we set up
between us and them,
whoever they may be.
But love respects no boundaries,
breaks rules
and reaches out across the barricades.

The need and opportunity together
triggered your compassion
to draw her in
where others would have left her out.
And she in turn
brought others in
to share the mystery of faith
she'd found in you.
A faith I share today,
perhaps because of her.
And certainly because of many
unnamed witnesses
who handed me along the way.
I thank you, Lord, for her,
and them, the unknown ones
who helped to make me
who I am.

Blue Hills, Cumbria

Love respects no boundaries,
breaks rules
and reaches out across the barricades.

Watercolour

Part Five

Facing the Unknown

Thimpu Dzong, Bhutan   *Watercolour*

Reading – Acts 9:43-10:27

Peter stayed in Joppa for some time with a tanner named Simon.
At Caesaria there was a man named Cornelius, a centurion in what
was known as the Italian Regiment. He and all his family were
devout and God-fearing; he gave generously to those in need and
prayed to God regularly. One day at about three in the afternoon
he had a vision. He distinctly saw an angel of God, who came to
him and said, "Cornelius!"

Cornelius stared at him in fear. "What is it, Lord?" he asked. The
angel answered, "Your prayers and gifts to the poor have come up
as a memorial offering before God. Now send men to Joppa to
bring back a man named Simon who is called Peter. He is staying
with Simon the tanner, whose house is by the sea."

When the angel who had spoken to him had gone, Cornelius called
two of his servants and a devout soldier who was one of his
attendants. He told them everything that had happened and sent
them to Joppa.

About noon on the following day as they were on their journey and
approaching the city, Peter went up on the roof to pray. He became
hungry and wanted something to eat, and while the meal was
being prepared, he fell into a trance. He saw heaven opened and
something like a large sheet being let down to earth by its four
corners. It contained all kinds of four-footed animals, as well as
reptiles of the earth and birds of the air. Then a voice told him,
"Get up, Peter. Kill and eat." "Surely not, Lord!" Peter replied. "I
have never eaten anything impure or unclean." Then the voice
spoke to him a second time, "Do not call anything impure that God
has made clean." This happened three times, and immediately the
sheet was taken back into heaven.

While Peter was wondering about the meaning of the vision, the
men sent by Cornelius found out where Simon's house was and
stopped at the gate. They called out, asking if Simon who was
known as Peter was staying there. While Peter was still thinking
about the vision, the Spirit said to him, "Simon, three men are
looking for you. So get up and go downstairs. Do not hesitate to go
with them, for I have sent them." Peter went down and said to the

men, "I'm the one you're looking for. Why have you come?"
The men replied, "We have come from Cornelius the centurion. He
is a righteous and God-fearing man, who is respected by all the
Jewish people. A holy angel told him to have you come to his
house so that he could hear what you have to say." Then Peter
invited the men in to be his guests.

The next day Peter started out with them, and some of the
brothers from Joppa went along. The following day he arrived in
Caesaria. Cornelius was expecting them and had called together his
relatives and close friends. As Peter entered the house, Cornelius
met him and fell at his feet in reverence. But Peter made him get
up. "Stand up," he said, "I am only a man myself." Talking with
him, Peter went inside and found a large gathering of people.

Imagine...

*It's noon in Joppa on a clear, cloudless day. The sun is high
in the sky. Feel its warmth on your back. Raucous gulls
wheel and turn, stitching the air together with the threads of
their flight. Scavenging black crows quarrel for scraps and
high above them kites trim their wings and float effortlessly
on the warm air currents. Behind you, to the east, lies a
jumble of rooftops, divided by narrow streets busy with
people and animals. The noise of the city is constant, an
unacknowledged and accepted background to life. To the
west, facing you, there's the beach and the Mediterranean,
blue-grey and restless.*

*Peter stands on the flat roof of the house, looking out over
the beach to the sea. The harbour is to one side, a main
entry port for the whole country. It's busy, a seeming chaos
of masts and ropes and seamen, carts and labourers. Ships
are loading and unloading, their cargo stacked along the
quay. Timber and grain, merchandise for the bazaars of
Jerusalem and all the country round about. There are fishing
boats too and Peter's attention is drawn to them, those on
the beach and other working boats further out. Peter has
never fished in the great sea, only on Galilee, so there's
much for him to see.*

The strong smell of tanning leather drifts up from the work yard below. It's different from the fishing smells Peter is used to but it's bearable. He moves from the roof's edge into the shade cast by a cloth awning strung between four poles. He sits down on a scrap of rough matting, facing south-east towards Jerusalem. He breathes deeply, composing his mind, and prepares himself for prayer. Slowly his recited prayers, learned as a child in the synagogue at Capernaum, turn to his concerns for the new believers, then become more personal.

The awning, the warm sun, the smells of fish and tanning, his hunger, all combine with the excitement of knowing that God is at work in Joppa, the Spirit moving among the people. Peter is caught up in it all, his early fear and shame at denying Jesus forgiven and forgotten. He is a new man, eager for new things, his mind open and ready for change. As he continues, the noises from outside cease to register. He enters the silence, his mind at rest, his whole being turned towards God. He is waiting.

In the heat the awning above him billows and flaps in a sudden breeze. It takes on a deeper significance in Peter's mind. His senses sharpen to the presence of God. He hears a voice speaking to him, preparing him for the messengers from Caesaria and the journey they will ask him to take.

The wind dies as quickly as it came. There's another pause and very slowly Peter becomes conscious again of the world around him.

He sits on, trying to grasp the significance of what he's seen and heard in his vision. Then he hears another voice from the gate below. A voice calling his name, insistent. Peter stands up and goes downstairs.

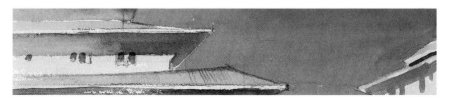

> At Caesaria there was a man named Cornelius, a centurion in what
> was known as the Italian Regiment. He and all his family were
> devout and God-fearing; he gave generously to those in need and
> prayed to God regularly.
>
> Acts 10:1-2

You'd know where you stood with Cornelius. He was a centurion in a
Roman legion, a junior officer commanding a hundred men. Higher
ranking officers often bought their promotion by family influence or
bribery but centurions were usually promoted from the ranks. They had
years of active service to their credit, and knew everything there was to
know about the army. They were experienced in command and combat;
used to giving and taking orders and seeing them carried out. No-
nonsense people on whom the army's discipline and effectiveness
depended. This was the army which had conquered and now controlled
much of the known world and was still pushing out its frontiers. There
must have been a confidence, a commanding presence, about Cornelius.
Not a man to be taken lightly.

He was stationed in Caesaria, the headquarters of the Roman army in
Palestine. It was a busy port, the main supply line for the occupying
forces, with several thousand soldiers and all the camp followers who
collect around an army. The Governor, Pontius Pilate, lived here – he only
went up to Jerusalem when he anticipated trouble. In fact his visits to
Jerusalem sometimes provoked it and he'd be glad to get back to the
sophistication of Caesaria.

Cornelius was no stereotype. There was more to him than a hard-bitten,
bluff infantry officer. Something set him apart. He thought for himself
and had a sensitivity to other people's needs that must have contrasted
sharply with many of the duties he had to carry out. He had a religious
streak too, something that probably provoked wry comments and rude
jokes in the centurions' mess. His mind was restless. He was searching for
something more than any of the contemporary religions or cults could
offer. Their pantheon of gods and goddesses left him unfulfilled.
Somehow in his spiritual journey he'd crossed the barrier between the
army of occupation and the Jewish people it controlled, had begun to
worship and identify with them. In his visits to the synagogue I wonder if
he'd heard the Psalmist's words, "My soul thirsts for God, for the living
God."? (Psalm 42:2) Balancing his professional and private life couldn't
have been easy. There was tension as he tried to work out his new beliefs
in practice and fulfil his duties as a Roman soldier.

He gets a good write-up in the story. We're told that he was devout, a man who took his religion seriously, not a common occurrence in the armed forces. At least it wasn't during my time in the Royal Navy. He was God-fearing – a term the Jews used to describe someone who wasn't Jewish but who worshipped with them and believed in one God. He tried to live out his faith in practical ways and was generous to the poor. And there were always many who needed his generosity. And he was a man of prayer. The fact that he was praying at 'about three in the afternoon' suggests that he was following the Jewish pattern of daily prayer. Three o'clock was 'the time of incense' when burnt offerings were made in the Temple in Jerusalem.

Devout, God-fearing, generous to the poor and prayerful. That's a pretty good commendation for anyone. A life pattern worth following. One that combined devotion and prayer with a practical outreach and – although it couldn't have been easy – as he continued to follow his life as a professional soldier. He was a man to respect.

Not always easy, Lord
to balance my loyalty to you
with all the pressures of my daily life.
I feel I'm on a tightrope, Lord
and fighting to maintain my equilibrium.

It's hard at times
to stand up for the truth,
refuse to make the little compromises
other folk expect,
cut corners, ease the way.
It's tempting to give in,
to swing to one extreme,
forget about the other.
To turn my back,
merge with the crowd
and go along with what the world accepts.
Expects.
That may bring temporary ease
but doesn't help to solve the deeper questions.

The cutting edge of faith is found,
not sheathed in Sunday morning services –
although I'm told I need those too –
but sharpened in the give and take of life.
Faith cotton-woolled in isolation
grows dull and blunt,
it needs a constant honing in reality.
So help me, Lord,
to keep the faith,
stand up for what I know, deep down,
is right.
It can be hard,
but then, I guess you know.

From Iona, Scotland
Pastel

A.D. ASKEW

One day at about three in the afternoon
he (Cornelius) had a vision.

Acts 10:3

I wonder what Cornelius was praying about. Prayer means very different things to different people, and takes different forms at different times. From written prayer book prayers, universal, beautiful and measured in language, to the spontaneous cry for help in a moment of crisis. For some, prayer means words, spoken aloud or not. For others it's waiting in silence, a surrender to God, a plunge into the mystery of his presence with no thought of self other than an overwhelming need to experience his love. Prayer can be all or any of these things and more. We can't set limits. It is our pathway to communion with him.

Whether Cornelius was simply reciting Jewish prayers for the day, thanking God for his blessings or praying for his family and himself, he was opening his life to the presence of God. A rushed prayer is better than no prayer but deep prayer can't be rushed. Prayer takes time and the regularity of Cornelius' praying helped to make him receptive. My guess is that there were times of silence in his praying. In passing, I question the sort of church prayer meeting where silence seems to be an embarrassment that has to be filled with words. If we want to hear God speaking to us we need to offer him spaces in which to do it. God's voice can be crowded out by too much speaking.

In the quiet Cornelius had a vision. Scholars have written about visions, attempting to define and distinguish them from dreams and trances. They don't help me much, and the finer nuances of interpretation leave me in a fever pitch of apathy. Vision, as a noun, basically means the ability to see, whether physically or through the imagination. However Cornelius' vision came, and whatever form it took, God was breaking into his life and asking for a response. It's the message that's important, not the mechanics; what God was doing, not how he was doing it.

The angel, God's messenger, gives Cornelius a specific request, along with a name and an address. "Send men to Joppa to bring back a man named Simon who is called Peter. He is staying at the house of Simon the Tanner." That's pretty detailed stuff, a powerful revelation. One thing intrigues me though. Philip, the evangelist who brought the Ethiopian eunuch to faith, (Acts 8: 26-40) travelled throughout this area preaching, until he arrived in Caesaria. He settled there and stayed for many years. So Cornelius and Philip were living in Caesaria at the same time. Maybe they attended the same synagogue – the early Jewish Christians still worshipped at the synagogue. Perhaps Cornelius heard Philip preach, even talk about Simon Peter who was visiting in Joppa just a few miles away. It's possible, but however the information got to Cornelius we can recognise the Spirit at work in Cornelius' life. The hidden presence preparing his heart and mind for the meeting with Peter which was to transform him and deepen his experience of the living God. And without prayer the vision might never have been grasped.

He's not the man I would have chosen, Lord,
Cornelius,
but no one is beyond your love.
There's room for all.
There has to be or I'd be left outside,
behind the door.
And if I show surprise
that you could choose Cornelius,
remind me, just as often as I need,
you chose me too.

You come in unexpected ways into my life.
You take me by surprise,
your spirit nudging in,
and often when I'm occupied with something else.
I suddenly look up and find you there,
a quiet presence waiting 'til I'm ready to respond.
No fireworks.
You are a whispering God,
not in the earthquake or the fire or wind
but in the still, small – yet persistent – voice.

I wonder at your patience, Lord,
the courtesy you show in asking a response
but waiting 'til I'm ready for a move.
You never seem to force the issue
and always I am free to walk away,
deliberately prodigal.
If that's my inclination I sometimes wish
you'd twist my arm a little more
and push me down the path that's good for me,
but that is not your way.
The decision's always mine.
Your way's a way of freedom
and though I've taken long to learn the lesson,
I know it is the only way.
Love can't be bought
and whether you are asking it of him – Cornelius – or of me,
it has to be my gift to you
responding to your gift to me.

It may surprise me that you chose Cornelius.
I wonder if he's equally surprised
that you chose me.
Perhaps one day I'll know.

About noon on the following day...
Peter went up on the roof to pray.

Acts 10:9

There must have been an air of excitement among the small group of Christian believers in Joppa. Peter was newly arrived there. He already had a reputation as preacher and healer. In Christ's name he had given life back to Tabitha (Acts 9: 40), and the number of believers was growing. Peter had decided to stay a while.

Joppa lay 30 miles south of Caesaria along the coast road and was an important sea port for the whole of Judea. A bustling town with a busy fishing harbour and many local industries, including tanning. Turning raw animal skins into leather wasn't a pleasant occupation and, in the eyes of orthodox Jews, contact with dead animals made its workers unclean. Little wonder that Simon the Tanner lived near the sea – the breeze would help to disperse the smells.

Peter was staying in Simon's home, presumably because Simon was a believer. Peter's experience with Jesus had changed his life, was still changing it, because the radical change Jesus brings is a lifelong progression. Already Jesus' teaching was working on the prejudices Peter had grown up with. He'd been among the disciples in their journey through Samaria when Jesus had welcomed the Samaritan woman into the kingdom he was creating. Now Peter was ready to take another step in overturning convention by staying in the home of an outcast. And with hindsight we can watch in wonder and fascination at the way God was preparing Peter for an even greater leap forward in his understanding.

Peter and Cornelius had some things in common. Both were men of action, each was a man of prayer. Like Cornelius, Peter seems to have been following the set pattern of Jewish prayer times (there's no need to throw the good out while rejecting the unnecessary) by praying at midday. Up on the roof of Simon's house Peter was watching the activity in the harbour and the ships at sea. Although he didn't yet know it he was sitting on the edge of a sea far wider than the Mediterranean – the great ocean of an expanding faith. The chill of the early morning had gone. Now the day was warm, the sun bright. Peter was hungry. His eyes closed. That comforts me when I think of the many times my eyes have closed, my attention wandered in prayer, although I can't usually excuse it by claiming a vision.

It was a strange vision but I believe God was using the everyday things around Peter to create the experience. The awning under which I picture Peter sitting became the sheet from heaven. The birds, the fishing boats and the smell of the nearby tanning factory, all combined with Peter's hunger to turn the imagery to food and an invitation to eat. But Peter was shocked. He said he'd never eaten anything unclean, although I wonder what he ate when Jesus and the disciples were staying in Samaria.

The real point of the vision had little to do with food. Often our dreams aren't meant to be taken literally. They are poetry, imagery, pictures with deeper meanings than appear on the surface. I don't go along with books of dreams and their superficial interpretations but we can sometimes identify a deeper truth in what our sleeping hours bring to the surface.

Peter's eyes were being opened to the truth that there was no limit to what God could make wholesome and acceptable in life – and not just at the dinner table. There are folk on the fringes of the church fellowship today who think they aren't 'good enough for God' or 'not good enough to be a Christian' – although a quick acquaintance with any church group would tell them clearly that neither were most of the people already there. It's perfectly true that we're not good enough for God, but that's completely irrelevant. None of us is good enough, none of us is worthy, but that's not the point. To put it in orthodox language – something I'm not very good at – Jesus Christ came to save sinners. As we turn towards him, for that's what repentance actually means, we are accepted as we are for what we can become. Not only is our future assured in him but he helps us to develop our potential.

God was telling Peter through his trance, or vision or dream, use whichever word you wish, that faith and acceptance have nothing at all to do with unthinking obedience to rules or customs or race and everything to do with the open-hearted love which Jesus revealed in his life.

Just another routine prayer time, Lord,
almost squeezed out by all the other things
that clutter up my life
and clamour to be done.
I come reluctantly with little energy
my heart not in it,
dutiful but nothing more.
I know the words, the good advice

that says when praying's hard
just keep on praying,
but that's much easier said than done.

I will admit it's no Gethsemane I face,
just the demands of every day,
the little things that still add up to little
when they're taken all together.
Sometimes I wish you'd intervene dramatically,
shred my complacency,
but visions never seem to come my way.

Perhaps it's better so,
at least you seem to think it is.
Maybe I'm unprepared,
not ready yet for all you could reveal,
and couldn't cope with more.
And yet there's something
in today's encounter I still value, Lord.
At least we're still in touch, still talking, you and I,
although the talking's mostly mine,
the listening yours.

I'll pause for breath and for a moment
try to look at things the way you do.
Forgive me if that seems presumptuous
but when I do I wonder what you see in me
that makes me worth the effort you put into it?
The answer once again is love.
Not mine for you but yours for me.
And in your loving look
there is a vision of what I can become with you.
Lord as this day wears on
and I wear on in company with it,
fan into flame the embers of my life.
I do not ask for blinding lights,
earth-shattering dreams
but just the gift
to see you in the ordinary.
To see the routine of my life transformed
in knowing you are in it with me
and I can do it all for you.

On the Beach, South India

When I find the time
to spend with you in quiet,
there is a voice that wells
from deep within myself
and offers me a vision
for my life.

Watercolour

> Then Peter invited the men into the house to be his guests. The next day Peter started out with them, and some of the brothers from Joppa went along.
>
> Acts 10:23

There are times in my life when God seems slow to act. In fact, there are times when he doesn't seem to act at all, but that's probably my fault, not his. Someone observed that God never does everything you ask him to because he leaves room for us to do something for ourselves, but (forgive the double negative) he never does nothing. God has his own agenda and timetable. It doesn't always coincide with mine, but in the long run I'm sure that his is the better. In the lives of Cornelius and Peter though God's timing was precise. Just look at the record.

Cornelius had his vision at about three in the afternoon. That gave him a little time to think it out and explain it to his servants. I'm impressed by that. He was an army officer, used to giving orders, but he took his servants into his confidence to help them understand the situation. That's good leadership. Then there was time for them to start out on the road to Joppa and walk seven or eight miles before finding a pub for the night. I assume they walked. They wouldn't have rated horses in their position. The next day, setting out in the cool of the early morning, they had another 20 or more miles to go to arrive in Joppa around midday.

This was the time of Peter's revelation, and the moment when he was sitting back and thinking about its meaning. Somehow, the word thinking doesn't seem adequate to describe how he must have felt – the wonder, the awe as he tried to come to terms with what he'd seen and heard, the search for understanding. And at that moment the messengers from Cornelius shouted for him.

Peter invited them in, 'two servants and a devout soldier'. That's all we're told about them. One thing we can be sure of is that they weren't Jewish. Jews were exempt from serving in the Roman army. They would have refused to fight under the Roman eagle – a graven image – and would have objected to any form of work on the Sabbath. That could have been a problem for the Romans in a war. It's also unlikely that practising Jews would have been willing to work as servants in a Roman household. This suggests strongly that they, like Cornelius, were Gentiles. They wouldn't have been welcome in a Jewish home, even if it was the home of a tanner. But Peter was already learning from his vision, opening his mind to change. I wish I could have been with them all that evening. We're told nothing about it but surely Peter must have met with Simon the Tanner and some of the new believers, and talked and prayed abut this new and strange opportunity.

However it was, Peter slept on it. A good thing to do when you're faced with a new idea, especially when it comes to you in a dream. On the third day Peter set out with Cornelius' messengers and some of the Joppa believers went with him. Did he ask them to go with him or did they decide for themselves that he needed some support? In either case it was a sensible thing to do. Friends can be a great help and Peter was going into a situation he knew little about.

As they walked towards Caesaria I imagine Peter thinking over his dream and its meaning. He tried to connect it to what he'd been told about Cornelius' vision by the centurion's servants. Peter must have realised there was a connection. Apparent random coincidences in matters of faith are usually not random or accidental, so what did it all mean? Cornelius' servants wouldn't have been able to enlighten him more than they already had so all Peter could do was to trust and walk on. Not bad advice for any of us when unanswerable questions crop up.

The group walked most of the day, staying the night on the way, and finally arrived in Caesaria on the fourth day. I wonder how Peter felt as he was guided through the streets of that city. A Gentile city, the headquarters and nerve centre of the Roman army. Soldiers everywhere he looked, the whole town geared to their needs. These were the conquerors, the oppressors, the people who had crucified Jesus, and now Peter was surrounded by them. In the lions' den, as it were.

As he walked along I'm sure his prayers were heartfelt. Prayers for strength and courage, for wisdom in the coming meeting with an unknown Roman centurion. Prayers that he would be open to whatever was to come and that he would find the right words to say. It's a situation that's been repeated countless times through the centuries, one many of us know personally at times in our lives. We can only do what Peter did – trust that the God who organised this timetable for Peter and Cornelius can do it for us too. Although just as God relied on them to make a response so he expects us to respond as well.

I'd love to have a vision, Lord,
a dream to call my own.
A startling personal revelation,
angels,
a voice that tells me
where I am to go and what to do.
A word direct from you
that picks me out as special,
an individual testimonial
that maps my life in miracle,
sets me apart.
Perhaps there'd be more chance of that
if I should find the energy and motivation
to spend more time in prayer as Peter did.
But that's a story I'm not keen to talk about,
not happy to confront.
Yet when I find the time
to spend with you in quiet
there is a voice that wells
from deep within myself
and offers me a vision for my life.
A vision of a figure on a cross
and then an empty tomb.

And then a voice that asks the question
"Isn't that enough for you?"

I'm sorry, Lord,
I'm just a bit obtuse at times
– and that's the understatement of the year –
but when I sit and contemplate your purposes
you draw me back in love to love.
It's love that put him on the cross
and love that took him off,
a love whose outstretched arms
embrace the world.
It tells me that I'm special
in a way that everyone is special too,
and that a word direct from you
comes every day,
a word repeated many times
that tells me to go out into the world
to love my neighbour.

And I hear a final question,
soft and persistent, asking
"Is that enough for you?"

> Then Peter began to speak. "I now realise how true it is
> that God does not show favouritism but accepts men from
> every nation that fear him and do what is right."
>
> Acts 10:35-35

And women too!

Their eyes met. Peter and Cornelius looked at each other with slightly guarded curiosity, the bluff, unsophisticated Galilean fisherman and the tough, well-travelled Roman soldier. Neither really knew why they'd been brought together although each had his hopes for the encounter, hopes created by their separate visions.

There would be formal greetings and introductions. Peter and his companions were welcomed, invited in, offered a bath and refreshment. The story doesn't tell us this, nor does it tell how they reacted to the offer of food and drink in a Roman house. Presumably Peter's vision would have guided the way they reacted to that. The narrator is in such a hurry to take us into the drama of the meeting that he passes over the formalities but I'm sure that's the way it would have happened. Then he was taken to meet the family and their friends.

The way in which Peter's talk is recorded makes him sound a bit self-conscious as a Jew to be mixing so intimately with Gentiles but he told them about his dream. How Cornelius and friends reacted to being classified as 'unclean' (Acts 10:28) isn't clear but Cornelius had probably got used to the terminology in his visits to the synagogue! As Cornelius responded with more details of his vision God's purpose began to clarify. The truth that Cornelius was struggling to find became clear and Peter grasped the startling fact that, in Jesus, God welcomes all, Gentile as well as Jew. Peter's mind cleared. As Cornelius found the peace he'd been searching for, Peter realised the road was opening for the faith to spread across the world. He took a sudden, dramatic and impulsive leap of faith, as great a leap as the time he identified Jesus as the Messiah (Matthew 16:16.) and grasped the moment.

"God has no favourites," he cried. A startling thought from a man who'd been brought up believing he was a member of the chosen people. A quantum leap in today's jargon, and Peter went on to preach the good news of Jesus. And as he spoke, the Holy Spirit took over in a mini-Pentecost. Peter was astonished but accepted without question the authenticity of it all. We're not told how long the celebrations went on, or how the neighbours reacted, but it must have been an amazingly joyful event. And we know nothing more of Cornelius, either. How did his faith change him? Did it make him a better soldier, or a more compassionate man?

God has no favourites. A startling thought for some Christian congregations today, a lesson we've learnt only imperfectly. We still fall into the temptation that leads us to assume and argue that my way, whatever my way is, is a better way than anyone else's. That my particular slant on faith is just a little superior to that of others. That's the sin that starts persecution and wars and Christians are not faultless. But superiority wasn't what Jesus taught, and not what Peter preached. All would be welcome in the new community of believers, although even in those days of great excitement Peter met strong criticism from the Christian brethren in Jerusalem when they heard what had happened.

Peter's actions – or rather the actions of the Holy Spirit working through him – showed that the door of the kingdom was open to all who believed, whatever their background. God has no favourites. Thank God for that because it leaves room for me.

Too much to take in all at once, Lord,
the wonder of your love.
The glory of its breadth and depth and height,
its never-changing power to recreate my life.
The force that holds the universe in equilibrium
yet finds the time to smile on me.
A love that meets the weakest link,
invites it to come close and never says goodbye.
A love that sees the possibilities in me
and if in me in everybody else as well.

There have been times, Lord,
when I thought I needed to be good
to force an entry to your kingdom.
Or if I paid attention to the rules
the gates would open automatically.
It was an uphill struggle, Lord
that left me gasping,
but as I paused, breathless and battered,
somewhere along the road
I glimpsed the truth I'd hidden from myself
– the door's already open wide,
the welcome warm.

I'm loved for who I am, just as I am,
because of who you are.
Past records are ignored.

It takes the strain away
and let's me concentrate on others, not myself.
The fight for paranoid perfection I can never reach,
unnecessary.
There are no favourites with you,
no special privileges that buy me precedence.
I come as others come not as of right or race,
or by genetic grace,
but through your open-hearted, open-handed love.
And if I hear you laughing gently
at the struggles I've been through
so be it.
I'll share the laughter with you
when we're face to face.

Thimpu Dzong, Bhutan

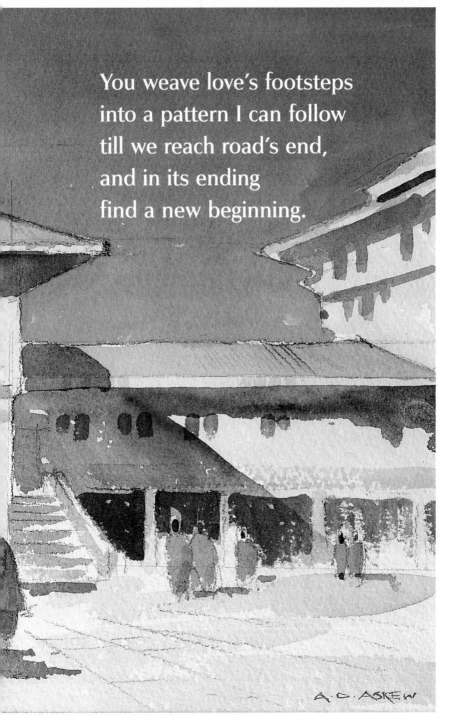

You weave love's footsteps
into a pattern I can follow
till we reach road's end,
and in its ending
find a new beginning.

A. C. ASKEW

Watercolour

Postscript

The stories in this book aren't just history. They are history in the sense that they chronicle the activity of God through the lives of people who lived long ago. But they are more than history. They are contemporary. The stories mirror your life journey and mine. They tell of a God who confronts us, as he did Moses, as we wander through our own personal wilderness. A God who offers us a clear sense of purpose. Not always a dramatic confrontation with a burning bush but a defining moment when we realise, sometimes reluctantly, that he has a purpose for our lives.

God refuses to give up on us. A God who in Jesus travels with us, refuses to let us go. One who crosses all barriers and leads us on into new, unexplored territory. "God," says Gerard Hughes, "is a beckoning word." And whenever we are tempted to feel we have arrived and know where we are, God dances on ahead of us. There's always more to come. He is inexhaustible. He takes us through storm and calm. At times he may seem to sleep or be absent but those are the moments when we grow and the seeming absences are our growing pains. He leads us into and through our personal Samarias, challenging our easy assumptions, our shallow prejudices. He opens our eyes to ourselves and our great need, not in judgement but in compassion, and opens our hearts to the needs and aspirations of others.

The journey never ends. It is exciting and frightening. In imagination I see the road we travel. People move along it, young and old, men, women, children. Walking sometimes in companionate groups, offering each other support and encouragement along the way, at other times alone. Some walk slowly, burdened like Bunyan's Pilgrim. Others travel blithely, in confidence and joy, dancing the road, but all head in the same direction. There are some who simply watch, unsure, yet even these are part of the journey. Not to make a decision is a decision in itself. No one may opt out. The journey is all-embracing.

Mark Tully, in Something Understood * writes "The journey is about risk and discovery, call and response, loss and transformation. It embraces and entwines our inner and outer reality, the spiritual and the physical, the solitary and the shared." And at journey's end? We shall not know until we get there but we are promised that it will be good.

Something Understood, An Anthology of Poetry and Prose compiled by Beverley McAinsh and introduced by Mark Tully. Hodder and Stoughton 2001

It's been an interesting journey, Lord,
and one not finished yet I hope.
You've taken me in ways I've loved
to places where I've wished to stay but couldn't.
At other times you've scared me stiff
by leading me down roads I didn't want to take.
On rutted tracks that seemed to double back
and led to nowhere I could recognise,
leaving me exhausted and unsatisfied.
Sometimes I've changed direction by myself,
found myself lost and had to wait for you, bewildered.

You've taken me at times down lonely roads,
on unexpected journeys when you weren't there at all,
or so it seemed,
and all my shouting and my prayers
– I think they're both the same –
bounced back unanswered and I was afraid.
But punctuating all the pain, so often self-inflicted,
I've known those precious moments of transcendence.
Times when I've walked the dog at night under the stars,
just you and me, and dog of course,
and looking up have felt the wonder of it all.
Have seen the light behind the darkness,
your presence in the emptiness,
lived in the paradox of kingdom here and now
and yet to come.
And through the continuity of time and love
have briefly and so richly
recognised your hand at work in me,
forming the deep desire I've felt, still feel, for you.

Yet still you move ahead of me,
rewarding and frustrating me by turns,
beckoning me on,
and in the dance
that's at the heart of our relationship
you weave love's footsteps into a pattern I can follow
till we reach road's end,
and in its ending find a new beginning.
All questions answered or made irrelevant
by the glory of our meeting.

The Leprosy Mission Contact Addresses and Telephone numbers

TLM International
80 Windmill Road
Brentford
Middlesex TW8 0QH
United Kingdom
Tel: 020 8326 6767
Fax: 020 8569 7808
friends@tlmint.org
www.leprosymission.org

TLM Trading Limited
PO Box 212
Peterborough PE2 5GD
United Kingdom
Tel: 01733 239252
Fax: 01733 239258
enquiries@tlmtrading.com
www.tlmtrading.com

TLM Africa Regional Office
PO Box 11104
Hatfield
0028 Pretoria
Republic of South Africa
Tel: 27 12 349 1904 x235
Tel/Fax: 27 12 349 2406
rashiraie@mweb.co.za

TLM Australia
PO Box 293
37 Ellingworth Parade
Box Hill
Victoria 3128
Australia
Tel: 61 39890 0577
Fax: 61 39890 0550
tlmaust@leprosymission.
 org.au
www.leprosymission.org.au

TLM Belgium (Leprazending)
PO Box 20
1800 Vilvoorde
Belgium
Tel: 32 22519983
Fax: 32 22519983
leprazending@online.be

TLM Canada
75 The Donway West
Suite 1410
North York
Ontario M3C 2E9
Canada
Tel: 1 416 4413618
Fax: 1 416 4410203
tlm@tlmcanada.org
www.tlmcanada.org

TLM Denmark
Peter Bangs Vej 1 D
DK - 2000 Frederiksberg
Denmark
Tel: 45 331 18642
Fax: 45 331 18645
lepra@lepra.dk
www.lepra.dk

TLM England & Wales,
Channel Islands & Isle of Man
Goldhay Way
Orton Goldhay
Peterborough PE2 5GZ
United Kingdom
Tel: 01733 370505
Fax: 01733 404880
post@tlmew.org.uk
www.leprosymission.org.uk

TLM Finland
Hakolahdentie 32 A 4
00200 Helsinki
Finland
Tel: 358 9 692 3690
Fax: 358 9 692 4323
eeva-liisa.moilanen
 @kolumbus.fi

TLM France
BP 186
63204 Riom Cedex
France
Tel: 33 473 387660
Fax: 33 473 387660

TLM Germany
Küferstrasse 12
73728 Esslingen
Germany
Tel: 49 711 353 072
Fax: 49 711 350 8412
LEPRA-Mission@t-online.de
www.lepramission.de

TLM Hong Kong
GPO Box 380
Central Hong Kong
Hong Kong
Tel: 85 228056362
Fax: 85 228056397
snelly@asiaonline.net

TLM Hungary
Alagi Ter 13
H-1151 Budapest
Hungary
risko.marta@freemail.hu

TLM India Regional Office
CNI Bhavan
16 Pandit Pant Marg
Delhi 110 001
India
Tel: 91 11 371 6920
Fax: 91 11 371 0803
reception@tlm-india.org

TLM Italy
Via Rismondo 10A
05100 Terni
Italy
Tel: 39 7448 11218
Fax: 39 7448 11218
agbertolino@libero.it

TLM Netherlands
Postbus 902
7301 BD Apeldoorn
Netherlands
Tel: 31 55 3558535
Fax: 31 55 3554772
leprazending.nl@inter.nl.net

TLM New Zealand
P O Box 10-227
Auckland
New Zealand
Tel: 64 9 630 2818
Fax: 64 9 630 0784
enquiries@tlmnz.org.nz
www.leprosymission.org.nz

TLM Northern Ireland
Leprosy House
44 Ulsterville Avenue
Belfast BT9 7AQ
N Ireland
Tel: 01232 381937
Fax: 01232 381842
info@tlm-ni.org
www.tlm-ni.org

TLM Norway
PO Box 2347
Solli
Arbingst. 11N
0201 Oslo
Norway
Tel: 47 2243 8110
Fax: 47 2243 8730
gaute.hetland
 @bistandsnemnda.no

TLM Portugal
Casa Adelina
Sitio do Poio
8500 Portimao
Portugal
Tel: 351 82 471180
Fax: 351 82 471516
coaa@mail.telepac.pt

TLM Republic of Ireland
5 St James Terrace
Clonskeagh Road
Dublin 6
Republic of Ireland
Tel: 353 126 98804
Fax: 353 126 98804
leprosymission1
 @eircom.net
www.leprosymission.ie

TLM Scotland
89 Barnton Street
Stirling FK8 1HJ
Scotland
Tel: 01786 449 266
Fax: 01786 449 766
lindatodd@compuserve.com
www.biggar-net.co.uk
 /tlmscotland

TLM South East Asia
6001 Beach Road
#08-06 Golden Mile Tower
199589 Singapore
Tel: 65 6 294 0137
Fax: 65 6 294 7663
cindysoh@tlmsea.com.sg

TLM Southern Africa
PO Box 46002
Orange Grove
2119 South Africa
S. Africa
Tel: 27 11 440 6323
Fax: 27 11 440 6324
leprosy@netactive.co.za

TLM Spain
Apartado de Correos
51.332 CP
28080 Madrid
Spain
Tel: 34 91 594 5105
Fax: 34 91 594 5105
mundosolidari
 @mx3.redestb.es

TLM Sweden
Box 145
692 23 Kumla
Sweden
Tel: 46 19 583790
Fax: 46 19 583741
info@lepramissionen.org

TLM Switzerland
Chemin de Rechoz 3
CH-1027 Lonay/Vaud
Switzerland
Tel: 41 21 8015081
Fax: 41 21 8031948
mecl@bluewin.ch
www.lepramission.ch

TLM Zimbabwe
PO Box BE 200
Belvedere
Harare
Zimbabwe
Tel: 263 4 741817
tlmzim@tlmzim.icon.co.zw

American Leprosy Mission
1 ALM Way
Greenville
S C 29601
USA
Tel: 1 864 271 7040
Fax: 1 864 271 7062
amlep@leprosy.org